KU-678-754

# CONTENTS

# DEDICATION

To all my students and clients who continue to teach me about the mystery of life and the majesty of living, my heartfelt appreciation and love.

To Darryl 'Jonathan' Harris and Beth Simmons Stapor, I am deeply grateful for the love and support I received while writing this book. You, my dear friends, edited, suggested and encouraged me to the very last word of the text. Darryl, a nurse and Reiki practitioner, provided invaluable contributions and insights into allopathic medicine. Beth, a Reiki Master, has a gift of clarity, enabling me to see if what I say is what I mean. Her feedback has been an important source of focus.

Here's to all my partners in flight. Thank you for reminding me that when we fly together, we fly strong, we fly high and we fly free.

# Part One

# REIKI
# ESSENTIALS

# 1
# INTRODUCTION:
# SHARED WISDOM

**I am pleased to be here** with you in this space of shared wisdom. Most people reading this book have something in common. We share a beautiful and deeply centring experience by being the instrument for this loving energy that is called Reiki.

Reiki has spread all over the world from the time of Usui, the father of Reiki. Many schools of thought have developed as a result and Reiki is taught in different forms. Modifications have been made to the traditional form of teaching 'to make it better', and many of the people who practise these different types of Reiki claim that theirs is the newest, best and most advanced. There has been some discord in the Reiki community as we try and figure out what is 'the truth' and where to take our stand. We are in a process, as a growing community, of surrendering into the energy.

Over the past several years it has become apparent to me that we tend to complicate our lives. We frequently have a simple and often profound truth and yet feel we need to make it more complicated and thus better. I have done this myself many times. However, I have come to realise that as we progress in our spiritual journey we move away from the need to define and separate ourselves. We return right back to the centre of where we started. We return to the essence. Being in the essence of Reiki enables us also to have the experience of oneness. Learning this simple truth has allowed me also to come back into the centre of my work with Reiki. I am encouraged to see more and more Reiki people realising that we can acknowledge and respect our individual unique qualities and at the same time celebrate the sameness. This holds true for ourselves as people and for all systems of Reiki.

If you have never experienced Reiki, then it is my hope you will be inspired to find out more about it by receiving a treatment from a practitioner of Reiki. It is one thing for me to describe how an apple tastes; it is quite another thing for you to have your own 'bite', which then becomes your experience. It is the same with Reiki. I am sharing wisdom with you that I have gained by being in the practice for many years. I encourage you to come to your own understanding of it by your experience. The more we practise this art and surrender to the energy, the deeper we will be able to work with others and to teach if that is our path.

I have been dedicated to teaching Reiki in a way that is practical and grounded. I believe that Usui walked on the earth as a practical and loving man. His compassion and willingness to be an instrument in an individual's personal healing was the start of a rapidly growing therapy. By remaining in the centre of the practice we experience the power and beauty of the system and ourselves. The work, as I see it, is one of deepening, being in the depth of our personal approach and our understanding of the treatment.

I realised, as I moved from using Reiki as a household art by treating myself, friends and family, to treating people in a Reiki clinic, that I wanted to have a clearer understanding of the majesty of the human being. My own personal search thus began this way. I came to an understanding that the work always starts within us. To understand others I first had to understand and know myself.

So many of us want instant gratification, instant enlightenment and instant answers. We think that by reading a book or taking a course we have then mastered something. However, it takes time to come into the mastery of this system and of ourselves. Therefore my approach is 'Slowly is Holy'. It is in the doing that we learn. The more we do the deeper our understanding can be.

I remember the first time I received a Reiki treatment. I am a very practical person, so when I arrived and saw all sorts of strange looking things in the treatment room I was put off. When I asked the practitioner about all the pictures on the walls and things around the room, her reply was that it was all 'New Age' stuff and helped the treatment. My reaction of distrust taught me something very valuable when I began my own practice.

I keep the decoration quite simple and make every attempt not to have things in the room that may conflict with others' philosophical beliefs. By giving everyone the space to relax they are more open to the experience of Reiki. I have a soft colour painted on the walls, adequate ventilation, a light-weight blanket to cover the clients as their temperature can fluctuate during the treatment, and pillows to support their head and knees. I have a lit candle and a beautiful bowl of flowers. Everything is understated and the room is designed for clients to be nourished and open. I play soft meditation music in the background, have tissues nearby, water for them to drink and the telephone is either turned off or switched to the answering machine. I am there for them.

The single most important aspect of the treatment time is listening to the client. Many people feel they are not listened to. So the very nature of your listening to them without jumping in with your own story or to answer their questions creates the space for them to feel they are important.

Also I watch the body language, how they use their voice and how open they are to touch. I listen and watch, then ask them, 'What is it you are wanting in this moment?' 'How can I assist you in realising this?' I explain that they will be using this energy to heal themselves on different levels. I also explain about disharmony. Basically, I paint a picture for their minds to see that reaction (i.e. stress) causes disharmony, and that Reiki will bring the body, mind and spirit back to its natural state. It is up to the clients to then make changes in their lifestyle to support this process.

I never have the answers for them, but I give them doorways to approach and choose to walk through. We may even discuss what was happening in their lives three months to three years ago, as emotions play such a big part in disharmony.

The beauty of Reiki is that it works with the cause as well as the resulting effect of disharmony. By understanding and working with your own personal disharmonies you will better understand them. We are a product of how we think and feel. If what we have created with these thoughts and emotions is not what we want, we can change that with the use of Reiki and also other complementary techniques that can be used with Reiki. Reiki can and does stand on its own as a valuable therapy, and is also complementary to other modalities including general medicine.

By asking simple questions, I provide a way for clients to look deeply into themselves. I make no demands as they look or discuss. The idea is to plant a seed of opportunity. It is then up to the clients to water the seed and encourage its growth.

When I ask clients how they are feeling during a treatment they usually describe a deep sense of relaxation. However, at times, emotions may surface. It is important to allow clients the space to release them. There is no judgement about their process. Gentle loving compassion and Reiki go a long way to reach deeply into the person so they can come back into a state of harmony.

When I have a question about an approach to something I will silently ask myself, 'What would love do now?' Most Reiki practitioners also have a support system with other practitioners to discuss the experiences they have when working with people and specific illnesses. Details about individual clients are kept confidential; instead we discuss the treatment protocol, and our reactions to what has taken place.

I keep records of all my clients, from their medical history and medication they may be taking, to response to the treatment. Then I note what I have picked up by scanning the body, my impressions and what other therapy I may have suggested.

It is important to maintain good relationships with the medical community and with other practitioners of complementary therapies. I would much rather refer someone to another qualified person if I am at a loss as to how to proceed with a client. Our aim is to work with the client to help them heal. We do not have all the answers; rather we work together for the client to discover what will heal them.

Reiki practitioners should be in a state of harmony when working with others. I take the time each day to give myself a Reiki treatment. By keeping myself in balance it makes the experience of receiving Reiki better for the clients.

I aim to be the silent witness to the clients' healing, acknowledge their work and be willing to be an example of how Reiki continues to affect my life. Many years ago one of my spiritual teachers said to me, 'Walk the walk and talk the talk'. I thought it was a catchy phrase. I know after many years of walking and talking that I have now come to understand that it takes commitment to set an example. I do not tell my clients to do anything I am not prepared to do myself. I am not afraid to not have the answer. Above all I empower them to be real, as real as – if not more real than – I have allowed myself to be. Only when I take off my own self-protective mask will my clients be given the space to do the same. I invite them into an experience of reconnecting to their divinity and magnificence. The rewards are great and my heart is filled many times over.

I wish you well in your journey to understanding the mystery and beauty of life through yourself and others with the use of Reiki.

# 2
# HOW TO USE THIS BOOK

**In this section** of the book I describe the systems of the body and the chakras, and the hand positions used in Reiki. You can cross-refer to this section as you read about the ailments described in Part Two.

Part Two looks at specific systems of the body and what results can occur when their function is impeded. There is a description of each body system, then the illnesses relating to each system are listed and described from both an allopathic and a natural healing perspective. Additionally listed are the glands involved, the relevant chakras together with an affirmation that can be used in the treatment, the possible emotional cause of the illness, followed by the treatment protocol or hand positions using Reiki and ending with other complementary methods that can be used in conjunction with the treatment. This Part finishes with a description of the complementary therapies that have been suggested.

The intention of this book is not to enable you to diagnose conditions with the use of Reiki. The idea is to bring you into a deeper understanding of the illnesses described and how to treat them using Reiki. It is for the Reiki therapist who already works with people, the person who aspires to be a professional Reiki therapist in the future and those who simply wish to know more about the miraculous way life is supported by our body systems, emotions and mind. The content forms part of the course materials used for the

Professional Level of Reiki being taught by myself through the International Association of Reiki.

# THE HUMAN BODY AND SYSTEMS

**The human body** is by far one of the grandest pieces of architecture known. Human life begins by the fusion of two single cells, one from each parent, which contain the architectural blueprint for human growth and development. The cells themselves are much more complex than that. They contain not only the blueprint, but also the foundations of life itself, that is life beyond the physical human being; it is life of the universe, of community and of the essence of the Creator. Thus, energy is the divine spark that awakens the cells. It is the breath of God within us that creates, nourishes, maintains and supports life. The cell is the single, basic unit of life. As cells reproduce and divide they begin to adopt specialised characteristics. Groups of cells, which combine together with like cells, are called tissues. Tissues also take on specialised tasks. They too join with similar functioning tissues to form organs. Organs have a defined set of functions to carry out. A group of organs, which have similar goals or functions, are called systems. The various systems of the body work interdependently to form the human body, or the human being. However, human beings are far greater than the sum of their simple yet complex components.

We are one in the ebb and flow of all that is. And the chakras are the power or the anatomy of the divine energy. They are the energy equivalent of the body systems. Our chakras are centres for reception, assimilation and transmission of life force energy. They are the master programmes that govern our life, love, understanding and wisdom, and act like a bridge connecting mind, body and spirit. It is not necessary to understand chakras in detail in order to transmit Reiki. However, the information that follows will bring about an even more profound understanding of the mystery and wonder of your body.

# THE CHAKRA SYSTEM

## The physically based chakras

The first four chakras are the physically based chakras. These form the foundation we build and stand on, and has everything to do with our physical reality. This is the start of our movement energetically into life and of defining who we are, who we must be in order to survive in the world and how we actualise our decisions.

**The Root chakra** (*Muladhara*) governs the gonads and adrenal glands. It represents the basic condition of our survival, all the fear, guilt and anxiety, the ground from which we rise above and out into life. A focus of our root chakra is our willingness to be grounded. The lure of materialism and self-obsession originate here. This chakra develops when we are still in our mother's womb and relates to our primary relationship. It governs the legs, movement into life and issues with our mothers.

**The Sacral chakra** (*Svadhistana*) governs the reproductive system, ovaries and gonads, and is our creative and procreative centre. This chakra harmonises our male and female energy. Our passion is carried from this area. Out of this chakra comes the fire that our imagination uses to actualise what we want, and the blind urgency for things that give us pleasure. It is also where we resist change and/or become spontaneous. This is the centre for our secondary relationships; father, teachers, friends and intimate partners.

**The Solar Plexus chakra** (*Mani Pura*) governs the adrenal glands and is the '*me*' centre, as it represents the beginning of our development of truly human qualities rather than the base energy of the first and second chakras. It is the centre of our ego and our need to define ourselves as individuals. It is the centre that is most actualised at puberty. This is where we come into harmony with issues of power. This is power from our personal truths and strengths, not power over someone or something. Will we be powerful people who empower others, or be victims or oppressors in life?

**The Heart chakra** (*Anahata*) governs the thymus gland and is the bridge between our physical and spiritual energy. It is the place for love and compassion. It is the love for others, our world, environment and ourselves. Compassion comes from an experiential understanding that we are all family and walk in harmony together. This is called oneness. To be compassionate is also to be detached from the outcome. Attachment is ego-centred. To be willing to be the instrument for the Creator allows a freedom for others. It is holding the space for others to have their own realisation. Our individual transformational work is to love and be compassionate with ourselves. This centre is normally more activated in our thirties and lasts into our fifties, depending on how well we have cleared past issues from our physical energy. It is a time to be more involved in community. We see the bigger picture of life because we are experiencing the true expression of our individual experience and unity with others.

## The spiritually based chakras

**The Throat chakra** (*Vishudda*) governs the thyroid and parathyroid glands, and is the centre for trust and communication. We develop the ability to discriminate between realisation and understanding. We trust our own deepest insight, trust others and communicate what is true for us. This centre works with the heart centre to actualise us in the greater world. We must trust to be able to be involved, to move away from our self-absorbing thoughts and reach out towards others. Therefore the key word for this centre is 'trust'.

**The Third Eye chakra** (*Ajna*) governs the pituitary gland and is the centre of our inner wisdom and intuition, where we can gain access to higher energy, our higher self, and can also live in a world with hope. This centre is part of our final stage of life when we forsake attachment to the material aspects of life. Certainly we may have material things but we also realise we do not need them to be who we are. This is where idea and imagination take hold, and are what we realise by creating with our second chakra. Dare to dream and you will create. The key word for this centre is 'hope'.

**The Crown chakra** (*Sahasrara*) governs the pineal gland and is our connection with higher forms of energy. It is where we begin to be inspired to live. It is the crowning of our spiritual nature and energy. The key word for this centre is 'faith'.

The task in our lives is to bring our spiritual energy into the physical body. When we have the faith to live, hope to dream and be guided, and the trust to bring what we know as spiritual beings through the heart of compassion and love, this happens. Faith, hope, trust and love give birth to our physical selves. We, then, become the lights of the creative essence who physically walk on the ground, having created ourselves as powerful people who inspire others to their majesty. It is a process of remembering our divinity.

The soul's light, the higher vibration of the infinite, travels through the body and is stepped down to a denser energy through the chakras and the endocrine system, which governs the body's functions. Therefore the endocrine system takes the energy of the chakras and refines it to support the physical body.

# THE ENDOCRINE SYSTEM
## FROM A
## METAPHYSICAL PERSPECTIVE

The endocrine system corresponds to the chakras. Each chakra corresponds to an endocrine gland. The endocrine glands are distinguished from other glands because their secretions are so powerful that they maintain a specific balance of forces throughout the entire body. If these glands become out of balance, our moods, behaviour and ability to handle things change as a result.

**The pineal gland** is involved with the perception of light. It produces melanin that actually translates one form of energy to another. It is the link between mind and matter. Through the pineal gland we are connected to the infinite. It is located at the seventh (Crown) chakra.

**The pituitary gland** is the guide of the endocrine system, and our development and physiological balance is dependent on this gland. It maintains all aspects of our growth, and is connected to puberty, fertility and feminine issues. It is located at the sixth (Third Eye) chakra.

**The thyroid and parathyroid glands** maintain our metabolic rate and breathing. The in breath not only brings air into our lungs but metaphysically it brings our soul light into the physical body. These are located at the fifth (Throat) chakra.

**The thymus gland** is connected with our ability to sleep and the formation of T-cells, which are essential for a healthy immune system. It is located at the fourth (Heart) chakra.

**The adrenal glands** are situated above the kidneys. They produce adrenalin, the hormone that enables us to deal with debilitating and stressful emotions in ourselves and in relation to others. They are essential for the maintenance of blood sugar and blood pressure. They also act as a bridge between what may be seen as the public and private parts of us. The chest is a public aspect and the abdomen is private. The adrenals are located at the third (Solar Plexus) chakra.

**The gonads** are found in the ovaries of the female and the testicles of the male. This energy ensures our continuation through reproduction. It is the grounding of our spiritual vibration, thus the end of the higher spiritual energy's journey into the physical body and the beginning of our rebirth into the spiritual realm. This is located at the second (Sacral) chakra.

From both an allopathic and natural healing perspective disease and illness occur when one or more organs, or systems, do not carry out the function that they are specified to do, when one or other of the body's systems begins to break down.

# THE HAND POSITIONS FOR REIKI TREATMENT

**Position 1** Sit at the head of the person with the heels of the hands placed over the forehead and the thumbs adjoining. Gently rest your hands over the person's face, allowing them to breathe easily. You may place a tissue over the eyes if you wish.

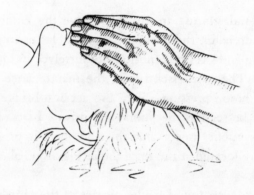

**Position 2** Sitting at the head of the person, place the heels of your hands at the centre-point of the crown. Your hands will extend down the sides of the head towards the ears. This position is often called the butterfly.

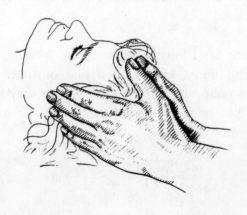

**Position 3** The person is lying on their front, with you sitting at the top of their head. Your fingertips touch the lower edge of the skull, where the head ends and the neck begins. Your hands are joined and placed on the back of the head.

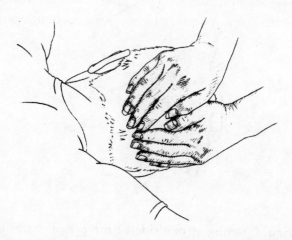

**Position 4** Sitting at the head of the person, bringing your hands slightly below the neckline, your index fingers and thumbs adjoining, and rest your hands on the upper neck region.

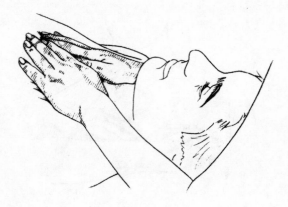

*Position 4 alternative* Sit at the side of the person, put the hand that is closest to the person on the upper chest region pointing downwards towards the lower body. Place the other hand pointing upwards on the other side. It will look as if you are making a semi-circle of energy in the throat region and upper chest.

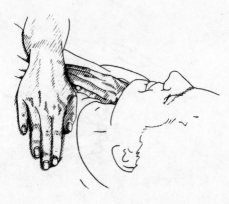

*Position 5* Sitting at one side of the person with one hand on one breast and the other hand on the other breast. You may also cup one breast at a time with both hands. If the person does not want their breasts touched, you may place your hands above the breasts so you are treating the person's aura.

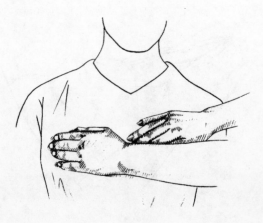

***Position 6*** With the hands one hand's width lower than the breast, one hand is placed under the breastbone on the right side and the other hand is placed on the left side, so that the fingers touch the heel of the other hand. Rest your hands gently on the body.

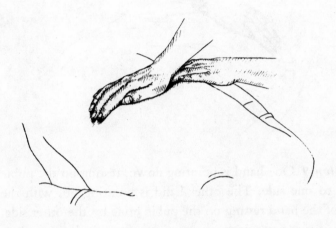

***Position 7*** Move your hands down one hand's width from position 6. Your hands will be slightly above the waist.

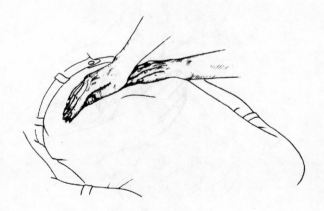

**Position 8** Move your hands down one hand's width from position 7. Your hands will be at the waist, the fingertips of one hand touching the heel of the other.

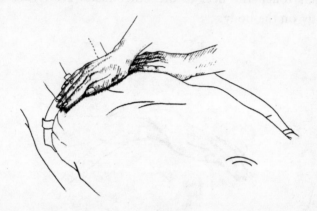

**Position 9** One hand is pointing down, resting on the pubic bone to one side. The other hand is pointing up, with the heel of the hand resting on the pubic bone on the other side. Note, it is not necessary to make contact with the reproductive areas of the body if a person is uncomfortable being touched there.

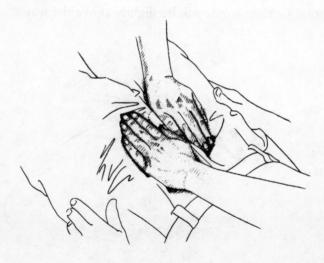

**Position 10** Place the heel of your hand on the shoulder muscle, with the middle fingers touching the channel of the spine. The other hand is placed with the fingertips on the shoulder muscle, and the heel of the hand touching the channel of the spine. (One hand is pointed up; the other is pointed down.)

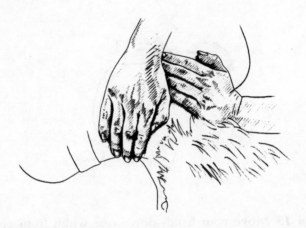

**Position 11** Move your hands one hand's width from position 10. One of your hands is on the left shoulder blade, the other is on the right shoulder blade and the heel of one hand is touching the fingertips of the other.

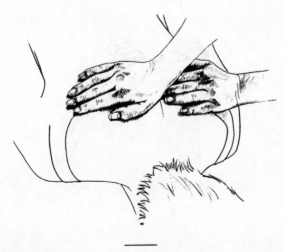

***Position 12*** Move your hands one hand's width from position number 11. The heel of your hand is touching the fingertips of the other hand, slightly above the waist. Your hands will be over the adrenal glands and the upper portion of the kidneys.

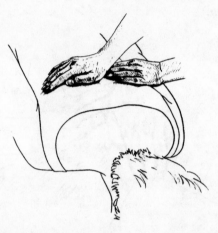

***Position 13*** Move your hands down one width from position 12. You will be slightly above the waist, with the heel of one hand touching the fingertips of the other.

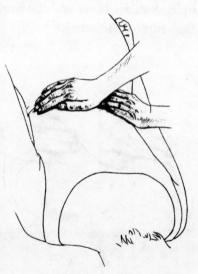

*Position 14* One hand is pointing down to the tailbone and resting on one side of the lower spine. The other hand is pointing up from the tailbone on the other side of the lower back.

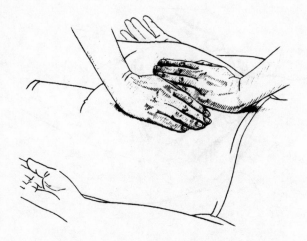

*Position 15* Place your middle finger gently on the ear opening. The middle finger will be bent to accomplish this. The index finger is placed on the head in front of the ear, and the ring and little finger are placed on the head behind the ear.

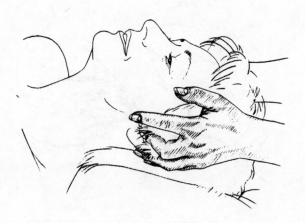

*Position 16* Place your hands on both sides of the jaw and over the ears.

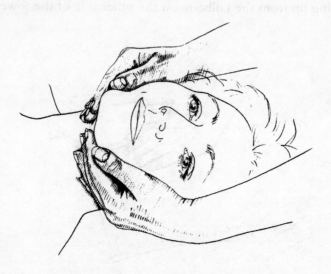

*Position 17* Place one hand on the back of the head on one side. The other hand is placed on the neck, over the carotid artery on the other side. Treat until the energy feels balanced and then place the hands in the reverse positions.

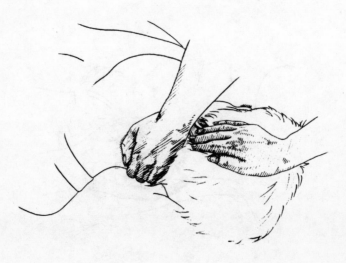

***Position 18*** Place one hand on the thymus gland, then place the other on the spleen, which is on the left side of the body. You will be balancing the third and fourth chakras together.

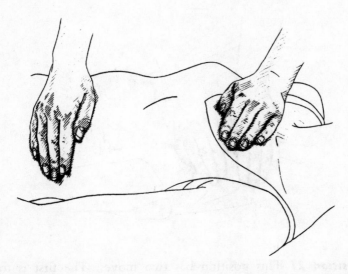

***Position 19*** Place one of your hands at the top of the leg, inside the thigh. The other hand is placed on the groin and the hands touch where the leg and body are joined together. Treat both sides alternately.

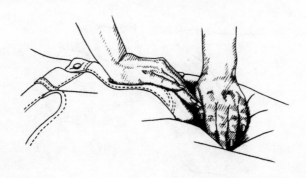

**Position 20** Place your hands under the arm in the armpit, using both hands. This is a wonderful position for clearing toxic build-up in the body and lymphatic disorders.

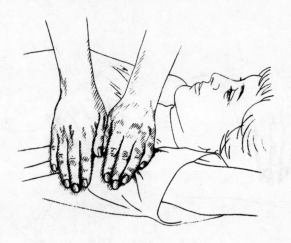

**Position 21** This position has two moves. The first is to place one hand down and one hand up on the person's upper chest as in position 4 alternative. The second is to place the hands on the line of the breast, as in position 5. You will then move one hand's width at a time until you have worked over the entire chest and lung area.

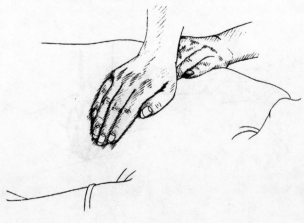

*Position 22* One hand is placed on the lower back in a horizontal position. The other hand is placed over the centreline of the base of the spine, with the fingers pointing down and the middle finger at the very end of the backside. You will be cupping the buttocks with your hand.

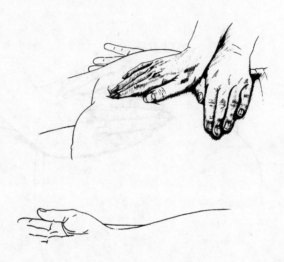

*Position 23* Place one of your hands over the heart and the other hand over the diaphragm. The hands will be touching.

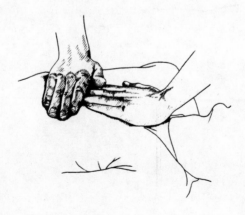

*Note: Positions 24 to 29 inclusive are used to treat the sciatic nerve.*

**Position 24** Place one hand over the sacral bone, with the fingers of the hand pointing down to the tip of the tailbone. Place the other hand beside it, with the fingers pointing in the opposite direction.

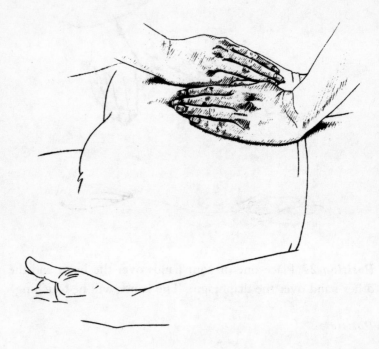

*Position 25* and *26* Move the second hand down the leg, one hand width at a time, until you reach the knee – *Position 27*.

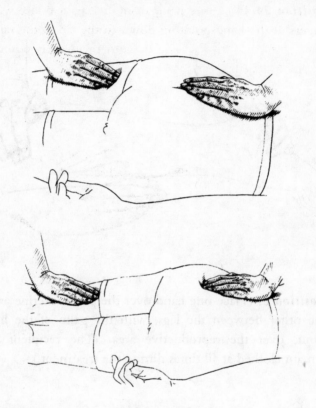

*Position 27* Sandwich the knee with both of your hands.

*Position 28* Using both hands run energy from the bottom of the foot to the knee.

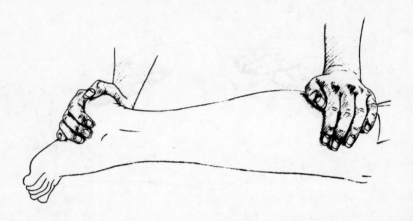

*Position 29* Place one hand over the pubic/uterine area and the other between the legs, with the palm of the hand in front, over the reproductive area. (The recipient should remain clothed at all times during the treatment.)

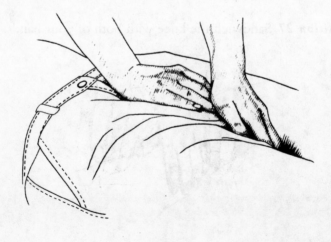

**Position 30** One hand is placed over the adrenal glands and the other is placed on the crown. This is to prevent shock.

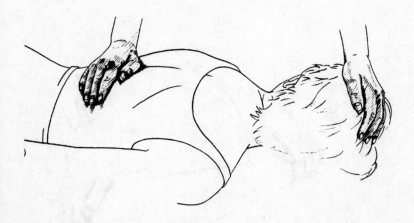

**Position 31** Run energy through the feet by using one hand on each of the soles of the foot. Treat until you feel the energy is balanced.

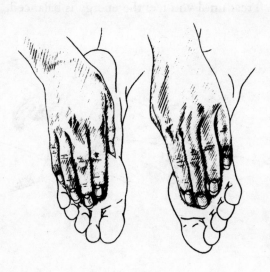

*Position 32* Run energy in the arm by placing one hand at the top of the arm on the shoulder area and the other hand on the wrist. Treat until you feel the energy is balanced.

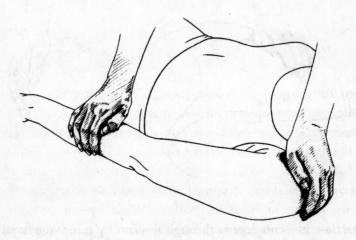

*Position 33* Run energy in the leg by placing one hand on the leg where it joins at the buttocks, and the other hand at the ankle. Treat until you feel the energy is balanced.

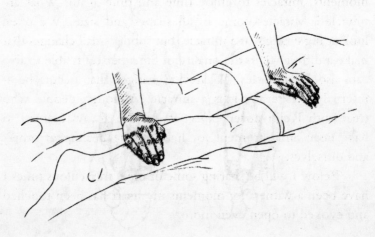

# 3
# SHARING MIRACLES

**Not long ago** I was asked during a radio interview what I considered the biggest miracle that I did with Reiki. The question took me aback, but I took a breath and said, '*I am not in the miracle business. What I am is a witness to other people's miracles. Because I make no demands on what they do with the energy, or how it feels to them, I therefore have no expectations. By having no expectations in my practice of Reiki I am free to experience the many miracles present in all moments. Many miracles come through Reiki but I am not doing them.*'

I honestly believe this. It has been my experience time and time again. When I do not expect a change and remain open to being the instrument, life brings me incredible moments, miracles to enjoy time and time again. What are miracles? Miracles come in all shapes and sizes. We often look at big changes as a miracle, but subtle, small changes that make a difference in the quality of life a person is able to live can also be miracles. Whatever changes that occur, be it internal or external, it is a miracle. Although people who treat with Reiki never expect it, we are always grateful to have been an instrument for healing, the healing of others and ourselves.

Below I will be sharing some of these miraculous times I have been a witness to; moments my heart has been touched and evoked to open even more.

# THE MIRACLE OF HANA

**Hana is a rare** and wonderful older woman who lives in a little village in Central Bohemia. She could only walk with the aid of two crutches and the help of someone in her family. Most of all she missed going shopping at the grocery store and working in her garden, enjoying the fruits of her labours. She also missed being able to get out and talk to her neighbours, to ride her bicycle and to play with her grand-children. Because of the problems with her legs she had been unable to walk unassisted for more than fifteen years. She stayed indoors except for the times her family helped her to sit outside. She was a very proud woman who felt defeated by life.

The day her family brought her to me she was using her crutches. The two people on either side of her seemed to be almost lifting her enough to move her legs, ever so slowly. It was agonising to watch her struggle to make it to my clinic. She had tears in her eyes as she told me her life no longer had joy or meaning. She felt like a burden to her family and wanted to die. I went to her, gently reassuring her and helping her to lie down and rest. I laid my hands on her legs, feeling the Reiki energy going deep into her. The legs that had been so cold and lifeless moments before became warm and started to be softer. I ran energy through these legs that had been keeping her from moving for so many years. I also treated her entire body. She instantly went to sleep. I suggested to her family that they massage her legs every day to improve the circulation.

I treated Hana five times and each time there was remarkable improvement with the tone of her muscles and her mobility. It became easier to get her to the couch to lie down. She said her spirits were being lifted, as if something was new inside her. She looked at me deeply with clear blue eyes and said, '*I have been feeling as if I am being held by angels. I look forward to the moments I can rest without any care in the world. I look forward to being here with you and Reiki.*'

On her sixth visit to me, she walked into my office with her crutches raised above her head. She had come alone. She told me that in the morning she walked to the store and bought her own bread and stopped to talk to her neighbour. Her eyes were twinkling and she said, '*Life couldn't get any better.*' I thanked her for allowing me to witness her healing. It was such a beautiful moment that I put on some music and we danced together. We were two grandmothers celebrating her miracle – she had healed herself. I knew that through this experience with her I would never be the same.

## JOHNNY'S MIRACLE

**I had been visiting** a family in the Scottish countryside. Just by chance their young son John asked me if I had problems understanding things in school when I was little. I replied, '*It's funny you should ask that Johnny. I was just thinking how hard it was to get my mind focused on what the teacher said and what I tried to read in books. It seemed like there was a part that was missing, like a door I couldn't go through.*' What was so synchronistic is that I had been doing some research into using Reiki with whole brain therapy. I had strong impressions about how to treat dyslexia and some motor neurological problems. I was searching for some people to work with to see if what I had been seeing had some validity. I went on to explain this to Johnny and his parents, and told them what I wanted to do. I asked him if he would be interested in helping me to find a way to help other children with the same problem as we had had. He and his parents both agreed.

I treated Johnny once a week for one hour. Instead of getting him to lie on a traditional couch or massage table I asked him where he would be comfortable. He said that if the weather was nice he had a special spot in the glens that was his and which he was willing to share. So off we would go with a blanket, something to drink, hand in hand, to his special spot. When I was treating him with Reiki he would talk about what he felt, how the energy seemed to move. He was full of insight. During the fourth treatment he became so quiet, I thought he had fallen asleep. I asked Johnny if he was sleeping. 'No', he replied. '*You see I am reading this wonderful book I found in the library of my mind, Mari. I have found the doorway to understanding. It's great in here and there are so many books to read.*'

My experience in working with Johnny became the foundation for some specialised integration work I did with Reiki. And his miracle of 'finding the door' has helped so many other people. Johnny is now a doctor practising medicine, specialising in neurology, complemented with Reiki, in his clinic in western Scotland. He tells this story to the children he works with.

## MARIA, THE GYPSY WOMAN'S MIRACLE

**I was in my clinic** in Kolin in the Czech Republic, late one afternoon, when a woman knocked on the door and asked for treatment. My translator said I was not available. I looked up and asked her why she was sending someone away. The translator replied that she was only a gypsy woman who would only bring me problems. I went out in the waiting room and brought the woman into my treatment room. She started crying and said she had a brain tumour and was going to die soon. Her head hurt so much and she was worried about who would take care of her children. I reassured her, saying that at least for this moment she could relax and let me treat her. She looked down and said, '*I have no money to pay you*'. I could hear my translator's silent words echoing in my ears, 'I told you so'. I said we would work something out, but 'First this is your time'. She continued to cry as she relaxed. I treated her body and then spent extra time on her head. It seemed to me that she had been carrying an incredible burden for such a long time. After the treatment she said again, '*I have no money to pay you*'. I told her that I wanted her to repay me by doing an act of kindness for someone else, so that she could be passing on the energy. I also asked her to come back every day so that I could treat her. After two weeks she stopped coming. I missed those times with her, although my translator kept telling me that it was good she was gone. I worked too hard and gave away too much.

One afternoon a little gypsy boy came to the door of the clinic with some flowers in his hand. He gave them to my translator and kissed her cheek. When he left I asked her what the boy had said. She looked at me with tears in her eyes, saying, 'He thanked me for helping his mother to talk to you, Mari. He said his mother was so happy each time she came from here because she knew that you did not treat her any different from anyone else. You had no feeling of judgement because she is a gypsy. She felt only love.' I asked my translator what happened to the mother. She said she was so shocked that she had forgotten to ask him.

That afternoon as I closed my office a man met me at my clinic door and asked me to follow him. He was so insistent that I come. I followed him to a little taverna, thinking someone must have a problem. When we went through the door the gypsy woman I had been treating met us. The taverna was her family's business. She had prepared an entire meal herself to thank me for giving her my time and Reiki. My translator was there and smiling. She said, 'Maria is not going to die; the doctor has told her that the tumour is no longer there. It is a miracle.' Then my translator said the biggest miracle for herself was in being able to see how narrow-minded she had been and that these people, especially Maria, had shown her how much she missed in her life by judging them.

## MARI'S MIRACLE

**I came to Reiki** partly out of curiosity and also a desperate need to find a cure for my own illness. I was born with a genetic spinal condition that caused lower back problems and in my early thirties I was already partially paralysed down my left side. Doctors told me that by the time I was forty there was a good chance I would be totally paralysed and in a wheelchair. My emotional and mental states were not good. I had thought of suicide and had been hospitalised for depression. I searched everywhere for a miracle cure, someone to 'fix' me. I was so closed to this, that I did not discuss it with anyone.

I was sceptical as I attended the Reiki 1 seminar. I also took the Reiki 2 seminar shortly afterwards. I was still not convinced about Reiki, but I transmitted energy to myself daily. At first I noticed that the depression had gone, and my emotional and mental outlook had improved greatly. Then gradually my physical symptoms improved and eventually the paralysis was completely gone. My mobility and health had been restored. It took almost a year to become completely cured physically, however I had been experiencing my life in new ways. Instead of being a closed person who did not trust anyone I was more open and optimistic about life.

The biggest miracle for me was not the relief of physical pain, but the relief from the emotional and mental pain that I had endured for so many years. I was truly experiencing being alive. I am still fully active with no recurring problems with paralysis.

## MOMMA GINNY'S MIRACLE

**Miracles can also occur** with absentee healing – a method taught in a Reiki 2 course.

While my mother was living in Texas in the US, she was diagnosed with cancer and given three months to live. My students and I sent her Reiki every day from the Czech Republic. She lived an additional five years with absolutely no sign of the tumour or the cancer. She was convinced that it was the Reiki energy that was sent from us that enabled her to live. Her doctor told her that there was no logical way to explain the miracle and in fact calls Reiki divine intervention.

When she died a year ago I sat by her bed with my hands on her, giving her Reiki. I was so happy that we had been blessed with the additional time together to say the things that could have been left unsaid – to forgive and be forgiven. It was hard to let her go and yet such an honour to be with her. She was so peaceful that morning in the hospital. She had been in a coma for four days. It felt to me as if she had waited for me to arrive from the Czech Republic, for us to have our last goodbye. We had some time together, then I put my hands over her heart and also held her hand. I remember saying to her, '*It is all right to let go. Look to the light, it is your time to rest in the arms of the angels.*' She opened her eyes, looked up, smiled and took her last breath. What a miracle she was in my life. She continues to be one of my greatest teachers.

It is such a privilege to be one of many thousands of people transferring this energy not only to people, but also to plants, animals and also to our world – loving hearts linked together witnessing miracle after miracle within others and within us. It is not the mind that understands, rather the heart that knows and we are touched by love.

*Part Two*

---

# COMMON
# AILMENTS

# 4

# THE
# CARDIOVASCULAR
# SYSTEM

**The cardiovascular system** of the body comprises the heart, blood vessels and blood. Its function is to transport oxygen and nutrients to cells, and to remove carbon dioxide and waste products from cells. It is also responsible for the regulation of heat and acid levels, responding to stress, and the control of bleeding.

The heart is located within the chest and pumps blood throughout the body. The right side of the heart receives oxygen-poor blood and pumps it to the lungs where it exchanges carbon dioxide for oxygen. The oxygen-rich blood returns to the left side of the heart to be distributed to the tissues and organs.

Blood vessels are distributed throughout the body. The two main types of blood vessel are veins, which carry blood towards the heart, and arteries, which carry blood away from the heart. These blood vessels are made of a smooth inner layer, middle layer and a tough outer layer. Veins are thinner and less muscular than arteries.

Blood is made up of three main types of cell: red blood cells which transport oxygen/carbon dioxide; white blood cells, which respond to infection; and platelets, which contain blood-clotting elements. Plasma is the main fluid substance found within blood and transports nutrients, chemicals and waste products.

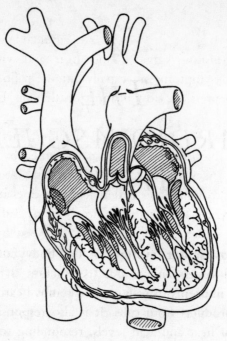

*The cardiovascular system*

Common conditions of the cardiovascular system dealt with in this section are anaemia, angina, cholesterol-related illness, hypertension, impaired circulation and oedema.

# ANAEMIA

According to modern allopathic medicine, anaemia occurs when there is an abnormal production, function or destruction of red blood cells. Red blood cells are produced in bone marrow and carry oxygen throughout the body. Used blood cells are destroyed in the liver. Aplastic anaemia results from low red blood cell production. Iron-deficiency anaemia, the most common form of anaemia, results from low production of haemoglobin (the oxygen-carrying component). Haemolytic anaemia is an excessive destruction of red blood cells. Megablastic anaemia is an abnormal development of red blood cells due to vitamin deficiency. Treatment varies

according to the type of anaemia and can include diet modification, transfusion, surgery, and iron and vitamin B12
supplements. Symptoms are usually fatigue, pallor, dizziness,
headaches, depression, slow healing, brittle nails, bruising and
palpitations.

Those who follow natural healing methods view
anaemia as a blood deficiency, usually caused by inadequate
nutrition or the inability to absorb nutrients properly. It is
also thought that the liver is deficient and does not produce
enough enzymes to metabolise iron. Many sufferers from
anaemia are older people who have a very limited diet.
Pregnant women may become anaemic because of the body's
need to nourish both the mother-to-be and the developing
child in the womb. Children who do not have a balanced
diet may also become anaemic.

## Glands
Adrenals

## Chakras
*Solar Plexus* Affirmation – 'I am willing to redefine myself
from a new perspective'

## Emotional cause
Anaemia is caused by a shortage of red cells in the blood. The
blood represents love and the related emotions of love. If we
have the opposite emotions such as fear, anger or resentment
unexpressed in our body, this restricted energy will cause the
liver to be out of balance. The liver is the organ treated in
cases of anaemia. The thoughts behind our disharmony may
be about our worthiness to receive love, a fear that we
cannot love too much, or we are not capable of truly loving.

## Reiki treatment

Treat the liver using positions **6** and **7**. I also work on the heart to support self-love. Place your hands over the heart gently, using position **23**. I ask the client to breathe into this area and let it expand with hope and compassion. Also, to stimulate the immune system, use position **18**.

## Recommended complementary treatment

• Eat foods rich in iron such as fish, egg yolks, blackstrap molasses, and dark green leafy vegetables like spinach, broccoli and cabbage. Also, eat foods rich in vitamin B12, vitamin C and vitamin E to aid in the absorption of iron and other minerals. Avoid coffee and tea and all milk products as they tend to reduce iron absorption.

• Keep a journal listing all self-criticism you indulge in on a daily basis. Substitute a positive thought for all negative ones.

• Meditate to become centred with the feeling of one's own space being enough.

• Bach flower therapy.

# ANGINA

According to allopathic medicine, angina is caused by insufficient oxygen supply to the heart due to narrowing of blood vessels by fatty deposits. It can also be experienced when there is temporary spasm of an artery, abnormal heart rhythm or narrowing of a heart valve. The main symptom of angina is mild to severe chest pain in the area of the heart. This is usually accompanied by a sense of pressure in the chest, which can radiate to the throat, jaw, upper back, arms and between the shoulder blades. It is treated with medication, diet modification, weight loss, cessation of smoking or, in serious cases, surgery.

For those who follow natural healing methods angina

indicates a deficiency of blood and energy to the heart due to a weakness of spirit and the absence of joy. Men get angina more often than women, as they tend to internalise their emotions, thus placing a big burden on their heart. Usually this condition occurs after the age of fifty.

## Glands
Thyroid, parathyroid and thymus

## Chakras
**Throat** Affirmation – 'I open myself to express all my emotions'
**Heart** Affirmation – 'In my heart I receive self-love and joy'

## Emotional cause
This ailment delivers a strong message to the body. You need to change the approach to the way you do things in your life. Instead of always working in the outside world and probably being very stressed, do things that will nourish you. Take the time to draw love into yourself and also love the people around you. Have you been so busy doing things, earning the money you think that you need, that you have forgotten about yourself?

## Reiki treatment
Use position **23** to treat the heart directly. Also use Reiki over the chest, positions **4** to **6**, and on the arms and back, positions **10** to **13**, to relax the muscles in the body and support the easing of radiating pain. If the pain is in the jaw area also place your hands on both sides of the jaw.

## Recommended complementary treatment
• Follow a diet of low salt, wholegrains, fresh vegetables and fruits. Also eat white fish and salmon, rich in polyunsaturated

fat, which have a tendency to reduce cholesterol and protect against heart disease. Avoid coffee, tea and foods rich in saturated fat.

• Avoid competitive sports. Try walking for about twenty minutes, after beginning with mild stretching. If the angina surfaces, stop and rest.

• Meditate twice a day for twenty to thirty minutes each time.

• Spinal manipulation and deep tissue massage along the spine will keep muscles relaxed.

• Do things for yourself. Ask yourself: 'What do I need to do today to bring more joy and less stress into my life?' Trust your answers and do what it takes to make you happy.

## BLOOD CHOLESTEROL

According to allopathic medicine high blood cholesterol is the underlying cause of arteriosclerosis and cardiovascular diseases, such as heart attack and stroke. It has no symptoms. Modern allopathic medicine regards an ideal cholesterol level as 160 mg/dl. Cholesterol is a fat (lipid) produced within the liver or absorbed from foods high in cholesterol (such as eggs and dairy products). Diabetes and hereditary factors also influence cholesterol levels. Cholesterol is used to make hormones (chemical messengers) and is an important component of cells. It aids in the transport of fats to tissues. Excessive cholesterol levels can increase the risk of atherosclerosis, and thus increase the risk of heart disease. Diet modification will reduce blood cholesterol levels. In severe cases medication is prescribed.

Natural healing methods stress that cholesterol levels are strictly dietary and are easily remedied by having a diet largely based on vegetable foods. High blood cholesterol is almost unheard of among people who eat a traditional diet based on wholegrains, fresh vegetables, beans, fruit and fish. Natural healers recognise that high blood cholesterol often leads to more critical problems such as arteriosclerosis if the condition is not controlled.

## Glands
Thymus and adrenals

## Chakras
*Heart* Affirmation – 'I am open to life and love'
*Solar Plexus* Affirmation – 'The definition of myself is continuing to change and I support it with healthy habits'
*Sacral Centre* Affirmation – 'I open freely to my creativity and passion'

## Emotional cause
In an emotional sense high blood cholesterol can be due to blocking and the inability to receive joy. There can be a real fear that when one is filled with joy it will not last; something will happen to take these good feelings away. Arteriosclerosis can be seen to have been caused by having a very narrow way of feeling and thinking. There is a hardening to life and refusal to see good in others and situations.

## Reiki treatment
Positions **6** to **8** to support the liver, spleen, stomach and upper colon, and position **23** for the heart.

## Recommended complementary treatment
• Eat wholegrains such as brown rice, barley and oats, dried beans, legumes, fruit, vegetables, especially leafy green ones, deep cold-water fish, onions, spring onions and fresh garlic.
• Avoid meat, poultry, eggs, dairy products, and all oils.
• Herbs to treat high blood cholesterol: garlic dried whole

5–20 g a day; garlic powder 600 to 1350 mg daily; hawthorn leaves, 80 mg twice a day.
- Meditation – Chronic stress increases blood cholesterol levels. Use meditation for creating a positive image.
- Use Bach flower therapy to treat the presenting emotions.

# BLOOD PRESSURE (HIGH)

According to allopathic medicine blood pressure is a measurement of force exerted on artery walls during blood flow. The force exerted varies according to the demands placed on the heart to distribute blood. Hypertension is an abnormally high blood pressure level. Hypertension is linked to age, family history, gender (higher risk in males), alcohol intake, diabetes mellitus, smoking (artery constriction), obesity (narrow arteries from fat deposits), stress, kidney disorders and pregnancy. Hypertension increases the risk of heart attack and stroke. Symptoms can include dizziness, throbbing headache, sometimes fainting, vomiting, visual impairment, convulsions and, in serious cases, coma. Treatment options include diet modification, exercise, weight loss and, in severe cases, medication.

According to natural healing methods high blood pressure occurs when the blood pressure is above a certain level that is considered safe. It is considered that stress is the single most significant factor, followed by disharmony in the kidneys.

**Glands**
Pineal, thyroid, thymus and adrenals

**Chakras**
*Third Eye* Affirmation – 'I use my intuition to respond in moments of stress'

*Throat* Affirmation – 'I am open to expression of emotions'

*Heart* Affirmation – 'My heart is open, I love others and myself in positive, supportive ways'

*Solar Plexus* Affirmation – 'The definition of myself is relaxed and responding into life'

*Sacral Centre* Affirmation – 'It is safe to allow my passions to be present'

## Emotional cause

It is thought that one of the leading causes of high blood pressure is a demand not to express any emotion that might be considered negative. All anger, frustration and sorrow are contained in the body and build up like a pressure cooker. So when anger is expressed it is often with such a force that it actually elevates the blood pressure. An occasional moment of crying will relieve the pressure but it will only build up again. High blood pressure can also result from long-standing emotional problems that have not been addressed. The cost of holding on to the emotional pain of the past has not been fully realised. When you hold on to what are considered negative emotions you also hold back on those positive ones. Holding on to fear or anger does not allow the full expression of joy and wonderment. Expression of emotions in a constructive and reinforcing way will enable the blood pressure to drop.

## Reiki treatment

Use positions **4**, **12** and **13** to support the kidneys, **17** to treat blood pressure directly and **23** for the heart.

## Recommended complementary treatment

• Avoid competitive sports. Seek games where all are winners. Use a punching bag as a way to vent emotions in a constructive way. Play water volleyball to hit the ball and let go. Swimming is good exercise and also will quieten the mind.

• Avoid red meat, eggs, fried foods and other high fat foods. Vegetarians seem to have healthier blood pressure than meat eaters do. Reduce or eliminate salt, avoid coffee and other drinks high in caffeine.

• Meditation – Do guided imagery exercises and chant daily. This will encourage the opening of the throat and calming of the mind.

• Bach flower therapy and aromatherapy – Use oils such as chamomile to soothe and relax, coriander to soothe and pine to promote relaxation and confidence.

## CIRCULATION PROBLEMS

According to modern allopathic medicine, circulation of blood throughout the body is impeded when veins and arteries become deficient. This occurs when blood vessels become narrow, blocked, inelastic, inflamed, thin or weakened. Hypertension, high cholesterol levels, diet, diabetes, smoking, excessive alcohol intake or injury can all affect the delicate structure of blood vessels. Treatment options include diet, exercise, medication and, in severe cases, surgery.

Natural healing methods indicate that stagnant blood and insufficient energy to the blood, heart, spleen and muscles cause circulation difficulties. The blood itself may be filled with toxins, preventing the blood from flowing properly. It is therefore important also to treat the heart and spleen when treating circulation problems.

**Glands** Thymus, adrenals and gonads

## Chakras
*Heart* Affirmation – 'I open myself to love and release all tension and toxicity'
*Root* Affirmation – 'I am fully supported in my life. I release my hold on to anything from the past'

## Emotional cause
Normally love energy circulates freely through the body. If we hold back on its expression poor circulation can result. When our legs are affected it could indicate we are not dealing with the issues that our present direction is taking us. We may be experiencing fear or problems and reacting by emotionally withdrawing from them. If the problem is in our arms or hands, it can indicate how we are not expressing ourselves or may indicate a desire to stop doing what we are involved in.

## Reiki treatment
Use position 7 to treat the spleen, position 23 to treat the heart, positions 19 and 20 to treat poor circulation, and 32 and 33 to run energy through the arms and legs.

## Recommended complementary treatment
• Significantly reduce fat, cholesterol and refined foods from the diet.
• Increase exercise by walking – an excellent way to stimulate circulation. A brisk walk for twenty to thirty minutes a day will also help pump the blood and detoxify the system. Swimming is also an excellent exercise.
• Use Chinese medicine to treat the spleen and heart as the underlying cause of the circulatory problems.

# OEDEMA

According to allopathic medicine, water is a major component of the body, and is constantly in exchange between blood and tissues. When this balance is impaired the tissues begin to retain water, causing oedema. This may result in a swelling of the affected tissues. Symptoms usually are swollen legs, and hands and feet. Systemic conditions involving the heart, kidneys or liver may cause oedema. It can also arise as a result of injury or medication. Treatment includes salt reduction diets and sometimes medication.

Before following natural healing methods for this condition, it is very important to have all other illnesses ruled out by an allopathic physician, as oedema can be a sign of a serious underlying disease such as congestive heart failure, kidney disease or cirrhosis of the liver. Oedema often indicates excessive consumption of salt, weak kidneys and/or a diet high in animal protein.

## Glands
Thyroid and adrenals

## Chakras
*Solar Plexus* Affirmation – 'I release all need to hold on to toxins in my body'

## Emotional cause
If the oedema is the result of kidney dysfunction it can represent holding on to fear that has not been acknowledged or expressed. If the swelling is related to the heart it can be about not expressing love fully for self and others. In whatever case, it is about holding on to some toxic thinking or feelings that need to be pressed out.

## Reiki treatment

Treat the kidneys and the heart using positions **12**, **13** and **23**. The swelling could also be the result of an injury. In that case run energy through the affected limb using position **32** or **33**.

## Recommended complementary treatment

• Substitute protein foods derived from animal fat, for low-fat protein foods such as fish and beans.

• Avoid foods high in animal protein and sodium.

• Use Chinese medicine to strengthen the heart and/or kidneys.

# 5

# THE DIGESTIVE
# SYSTEM

**The digestive system comprises** the digestive tract and associated digestive organs. The function of the digestive tract is to break down dietary food into simple chemicals (digestive process) for use by the body as energy, and for maintaining tissues and cells. The digestive tract consists of the mouth, pharynx (throat), oesophagus (gullet), stomach, small intestines (duodenum, jejunum, ileum), large intestines (caecum, colon, rectum) and anus. The associated digestive organs are the salivary glands, liver, gallbladder and pancreas. These organs secrete chemicals, which aid in the breakdown of food. Food passes through the digestive tract as the intestinal walls expand and contract in a wave-like motion known as peristalsis.

## THE DIGESTIVE PROCESS

The food we eat contains elements essential for the body to function efficiently. It is made up of nutrients, vitamins, minerals, carbohydrates, proteins, fats, fibre and water. These must be broken down into smaller particles before they can be absorbed and used by the body. This process is called the digestive process. The digestive process begins in the mouth. Teeth break down food into small balls (boli) which can pass easily down the digestive tract. Saliva is secreted by salivary glands into the mouth and lubricates the boli as well as

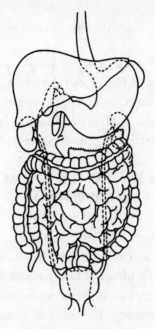

*The digestive system*

commencing the breakdown of carbohydrates. Boli then pass into the stomach via the pharynx and oesophagus. In the stomach the food particles continue to be broken down mechanically through muscle activity in the stomach. The lining of the stomach produces acid (hydrochloric acid) and a protein-digesting enzyme (pepsin) which chemically break down food particles. The now semi-liquid product passes into the duodenum, and salts, acids and digestive enzymes produced by the gallbladder and pancreas are released into the duodenum to continue the breakdown of carbohydrates, fats and proteins. The walls of the small intestine now absorb the products of digestion into the bloodstream and lymphatic system for transportation throughout the body. The remainder of the liquid is passed into the large intestine where water is reabsorbed via the walls of the colon. Left-over products of digestion are then excreted from the body via the rectum and anus as faeces. The digestive process can take from ten hours to several days.

Common disorders of the digestive system dealt with in this section are canker sores, colic, colitis, constipation, diarrhoea, dyspepsia, flatulence, gallbladder disease, halitosis, haemorrhoids, hepatitis, teeth and gum disorders, ulcers.

# CANKER SORES (MOUTH ULCERS)

According to modern allopathic medicine, canker sores are caused by a break in the lining of the mouth and are often referred to as mouth ulcers. They are painful, usually round and can be yellow, grey or white in colour with a red, inflamed surrounding. Commonly the herpes simplex virus causes these ulcers, but rarely it indicates an underlying problem such as anaemia, syphilis, mouth cancer or tuberculosis. Treatment is symptomatic, usually with mouth washes and medication.

Natural healing methods state that canker sores are a discharge of waste that is not being cleansed by the liver and kidneys. This means that canker sores indicate depressed liver and kidney function. Treatment is usually to strengthen the liver and kidneys so that the blood can be more easily cleansed.

## Glands
Adrenals and ovaries (in premenstrual women)

## Chakras
*Solar Plexus* Affirmation – 'I release all toxins that I have been holding on to'

**Emotional cause**
The mouth acts as a gateway where we take in things to assimilate. Canker sores can be demonstrating that what we have taken in has caused us to react with irritation. The mouth is also where we express ourselves, so conflict could be occurring as a result of non-communication, our words festering in our mouths.

**Reiki treatment**
Use positions **12**, **13** and **7** to strengthen the liver and kidneys. If the sore has occurred in a premenstrual woman, then use position **9** to work with the ovaries. You can also place a gauze bandage on the sore and Reiki directly the area where the sore is.

**Recommended complementary treatment**
• Avoid dairy products, oily foods, sweets, salty foods and animal protein.
• Liver detoxification – do a one-to-three-day carrot juice fast to cleanse the liver. Juice fresh carrots and drink six to eight glasses each day.
• At the first sign of the sore apply a wet black tea bag to the ulcer – tannin is an astringent with pain-relieving qualities.

# COLIC (INFANTILE)

According to modern allopathic medicine, infantile colic is a painful spasmodic contraction of the intestine, which is probably caused by obstruction of the intestine. The symptoms of colic in infants are abdominal pain, distension, restlessness, insomnia and crying. Babies will often be irritable and screaming. They will pull up their legs, suggesting pain in the abdomen, quite often passing gas. The symptoms may worsen at night. Treatment is not usually required but medication may be prescribed in severe cases.

According to natural healing methods, colic occurs when an infant's digestive system is not able to fully assimilate and eliminate the food it is being fed, whether it is mother's milk or a bottle of formula. With breast-fed babies what the mother is eating is of great importance and can be the cause of the problem. Formula-fed babies may be allergic to the milk. In such cases vitamin-enriched goat's milk may be the answer, but check with your doctor before trying this.

## Glands
Adrenals

## Chakras
*Solar Plexus* Affirmation – 'I am taking in nourishment and growing with a clear definition of my world and myself'

## Emotional cause
It may be that the baby has become annoyed with its surroundings and is irritable. The baby could be impatient to get on with living and is mentally gulping at life.

## Reiki treatment
When the baby has eaten, place a hand over its diaphragm using Reiki and also slowly rock the child so that it will burp. Use positions **6** and **7** to work with the solar plexus.

## Recommended complementary treatment
• Substitute the baby's formula with vitamin-enriched goat's milk, perhaps diluted with boiled water.
• Carry the baby in a front sling so that it is cuddled up close to its mother and feels her warmth.
• If the mother is under stress, treat this, as the baby may be reacting to the mother's feelings.

# COLITIS

According to modern allopathic medicine, colitis is an infection of the colon which results in abdominal pain, fever, and diarrhoea with blood and mucus. It is caused either by foreign bacterial growth, viruses, a decrease in bacteria normally resident in the colon or dead colon tissue. It may also indicate ulcerative colitis or Crohn's disease. Treatment in most cases is unnecessary, but medication and occasionally surgery may be required.

In natural healing methods colitis is considered to be 'a civilised disease' because of the dietary influence of the West. Traditionally diet is regarded as the central cause of the illness; another is lack of exercise.

## Glands
Adrenals

## Chakras
*Solar Plexus* Affirmation – 'I release all irritation. I experience myself in new, calm ways'
*Sacral Centre* Affirmation – 'I am in balance with myself'

## Emotional cause
Colitis is seen as an erupted emotional state relating to acceptance and digesting the reality of what is taking place in our lives. This includes the events that are happening and our relationships. The colon is concerned with dealing with things in the relative world. When colitis has progressed to an ulcerous state this irritation has become so intense that it is finally eating away at us. This indicates a change in attitude.

## Reiki treatment
Use positions **5** to **7** to treat the solar plexus and sacral centre.

## Recommended complementary treatment
• Follow a diet that is rich in high fibre and low protein for the best prevention and cure. If the symptoms are bad it is best to introduce fibre very slowly so as not to exacerbate the symptoms.
• T'ai chi is a simple and yet profound movement that calms the mind and will reduce stress.
• Meditation will relax the body and mind. Use simple breathing techniques to reduce stress.
• Bach flower therapy.

# CONSTIPATION

Modern allopathic medicine describes constipation as the passing of hard, dry, infrequent faeces. According to allopathic medicine, headaches, a coated tongue and a sense of tiredness, bad breath and depression often accompany constipation. Lack of fibre in the diet, but occasionally an underlying condition, mostly cause constipation. Increasing dietary fibre, water intake and regular exercise can aid in the management of constipation. Laxatives should be avoided.

Natural healing methods state that the main cause of constipation is a fibre-deficient diet, and also a weakened spleen. If constipation has been a long-standing problem the bowels must be re-educated and strengthened.

## Glands
Adrenals

## Chakras
*Solar Plexus* Affirmation – 'I freely let go of all that I am holding on to. I release all fear, anxiety and need to control'
*Sacral Centre* Affirmation – 'I release all toxins and toxic thoughts and feelings. I move with the natural flow of life'

## Emotional cause

Constipation is seen as a way to control events. It also indicates a lack of spontaneity. It shows inflexibility and a reluctance to go with the flow. It may be that we have a feeling of being powerless and insecure that has kept us holding on to what we do know. We are afraid of the unknown and of living fully.

## Reiki treatment

Use position **8** to work with the colon.

## Recommended complementary treatment

• Follow a high fibre diet consisting of green, leafy vegetables and wholegrains. Also eat plenty of raw fruit and vegetables. Drink four to eight glasses of purified water every day.
• Use acupressure massage to strengthen the meridians of the spleen.
• Shiatsu massage will strengthen the spleen meridian.
• Bowen body therapy will open the energy of the abdomen.
• Taking a brisk daily walk will stimulate and strengthen the abdominal muscles and also promote healthy intestinal function.
• Stretching exercises and yoga.
• Bach flower therapy.

# DIARRHOEA

According to modern allopathic medicine, diarrhoea is the passing of frequent, watery, voluminous faeces. Generally a bout of diarrhoea is caused by eating infected food, although chronic diarrhoea may be an indication of an underlying disease (e.g. Crohn's, ulcerative colitis or irritable bowel syndrome). The major concern with diarrhoea is the loss of body fluid and salts. These can be replaced by drinking plenty of water and salt replacement mixtures. Diarrhoea in children can be hazardous and should always be referred to a physician.

Those who follow natural healing methods view diarrhoea as the body's normal reaction to the presence of a toxic agent. It is an efficient way to eliminate viruses, bacteria and toxic foods from the body. Chronic diarrhoea in most cases is due to a weakness in the digestive system, which includes the spleen, stomach, pancreas, liver, gallbladder, and small and large intestines.

## Glands
Adrenals

## Chakras
**Solar Plexus** Affirmation – 'I release my need to control, and allow life to move through me'
**Sacral Centre** Affirmation – 'I am in alignment with all aspects of my personality and passion'

## Emotional cause
Diarrhoea can indicate a type of person who does not slow down and does not listen to their body's wisdom. They do not take the time to integrate and assimilate. Sometimes what we experience in life is too overwhelming to absorb.

## Reiki treatment
Treat using positions **6** to **8**.

## Recommended complementary treatment
• Avoid honey, spinach, cows' milk, apricots, plums, sesame seeds, and any foods that are difficult to digest.
• Homoeopathy – Arsenicum: if the stomach feels heavy and

nausea is present; Cuprum arsenicosum: for burning and cramping colicky pain; Gersemium: for diarrhoea caused by anticipation or fear; and sulphur: for changeable stools. Consult a qualified homoeopathic practitioner.
• Journal writing is especially recommended when stress is the most possible cause of the problem. This allows you to write out what is bothering you.
• Meditation uses the breath to relax deeply. Do this twice a day for approximately ten minutes each time.
• Use massage for relaxation.
• Bach flower therapy.

# DYSPEPSIA (INDIGESTION)

According to modern allopathic medicine, dyspepsia is frequently experienced as heartburn, abdominal pain, nausea or flatulence. It is usually caused by eating too much too quickly, and spicy or rich food. It may also be caused by stress. Proper eating habits will combat dyspepsia. Milk and medications can reduce the effects of indigestion.

Natural healing methods indicate that poor food combinations and emotional upset cause dyspepsia.

## Glands
Adrenals

## Chakras
*Solar Plexus* Affirmation – 'I open and flow with life'
*Sacral Centre* Affirmation – 'I am in harmony with my passion and sexuality'

## Emotional cause
We may feel we have lost control of what is happening in our lives. The reality we are dealing with and taking in is creating

some upset and disharmony within. We need to look at what we are reluctant to assimilate or digest in our lives.

## Reiki treatment
Treat using positions **6** to **8**.

## Recommended complementary treatment
• Use food combining to encourage proper assimilation and elimination: eat simpler meals; eat protein and starch at separate meals. Only eat protein with leafy, green vegetables. Fruits and sweetened foods should be eaten alone.
• Foods to aid digestion include apples, barley, grapefruit peel, lemons, limes and carrots.
• Avoid eating meat, dairy products, eggs, poor quality oils, sugar, spicy foods, fried foods and alcohol.
• Meditation – for visualisation and relaxation. To come into harmony with the ebb and flow of life moving through you and nourishing you.
• Bach flower therapy.

# FLATULENCE (GAS PAIN)

According to modern allopathic medicine, flatulence is a painful build-up of gas in the digestive tract, resulting from indigestion, irritable bowel syndrome or gallbladder disorders. Gas is passed through the digestive tract and out the anus. Treatment is not generally required. Avoidance of carbonated drinks may help.

According to natural healing methods the cause of intestinal gas is fermented foods. It is thought that these foods are partially digested due to an imbalance in the digestive system and in particular the spleen. The spleen is the organ that supplies life-force energy to the small and large intestines. If the spleen is weakened, then there will be insufficient energy to digest the food properly. Coupled with this is the type of food that is being digested. High amounts of animal protein, beans, dairy products and gluten require more time and work to digest. Constipation is also a cause of flatulence.

## Glands
Adrenals

## Chakras
*Solar Plexus* Affirmation – 'I easily digest and integrate all thoughts, feelings and substances. I flow with life'

## Emotional cause
Flatulence with pain can represent gripping fear, undigested ideas and feelings. If you suffer from flatulence ask yourself these questions: What are you holding on to that is fermenting not only in your body but in your mind? What part of you is not ready to let go and flow in the stream of life? Where is the struggle in your life and when will you decide to release it?

## Reiki treatment
Treat the spleen and digestive areas using positions **6** to **8**.

## Recommended complementary treatment
• Eat slowly and chew your food; do not drink liquids with your meals; and wait at least ten to twenty minutes after eating before drinking. Do not eat when under stress.
• Eat lemon and lime to aid digestion, also bitter foods such as romaine lettuce, asparagus, radish leaves, watercress and alfalfa which help the body to assimilate animal protein.
• Avoid fried foods, sugar, junk food, poor food combining and ice-cold drinks.
• Use meditation to calm the mind and settle the stress levels in the body.

• Homoeopathy – Chamomilla: for an abdomen distended with gas; Carbo vegetablis: for gas and belching about half-an-hour after eating. Consult a qualified homoeopathic practitioner.
• Bach flower therapy.

# GALLBLADDER DISEASE

According to modern allopathic medicine, the gallbladder aids in the digestion of food by secreting enzymes and chemicals into the duodenum. The most common cause of gallbladder problems is the formation of gallstones which can cause pain as they pass out of the gallbladder into the common bile duct. Inflammation of the gallbladder may arise from gallstones constricting the gallbladder outlet. Symptoms may include: headaches, irritability, quick temper, chronic constipation, fever and chills. Severe cases are treated with surgery.

For those who follow natural healing methods, gallbladder disease and gallstones are the result of a western diet that is high in fats and cholesterol. Once fat and cholesterol are at normal levels, then the bile acids and detergents work naturally to dissolve any stones that remain inside the gallbladder.

**Glands**
Adrenals

**Chakras**
*Solar Plexus* Affirmation – 'I release my past with joy'
*Sacral Centre* Affirmation – 'I open to the creative forces within me'

## Emotional cause

The bile in the gallbladder represents any bitterness that we have held on to. Ask yourself: Where is your resentment and anger? Is it turned towards you or others? Does the anger and resentment remain unexpressed? Are you frustrated with life and others? If you find yourself answering 'yes' to any of these questions perhaps it is time to let go and forgive, and allow sweetness into your life.

## Reiki treatment

Treat the liver, spleen and intestines with positions **6** to **8**, **12** and **13**.

## Recommended complementary treatment

• Eat olive oil at least five times a week to cleanse the gallbladder. Drink apple juice, red beetroot juice, grapefruit juice or carrot juice.
• Avoid meat, eggs, refined carbohydrates, nuts and peanut butter, sugar, alcohol and dairy products.
• Edgar Casey recommends that you massage olive oil into the area of the gallbladder and liver.
• Use acupressure or acupuncture treatment to stimulate the liver and gallbladder meridians.
• Bach flower therapy.

# HAEMORRHOIDS

According to modern allopathic medicine, haemorrhoids are a swelling of a vein or veins within the anus, usually caused by excessive pressure placed on the veins, such as during pregnancy and chronic constipation. Fluids and high fibre diets can aid in the management of haemorrhoids. Occasionally medication and/or surgery may be required.

Natural healing methods indicate that the spleen is not

balanced which causes the spleen to contract and send a rush of blood into the vessels. Some of these vessels swell beyond their normal limit within the tissue and cause haemorrhoids. It goes without saying that diet plays a large part in this condition. Too much fat and sugar with little fibre will exacerbate the problem.

## Glands
Adrenals and gonads

## Chakras
*Solar Plexus* Affirmation – 'I am open to receive and to give'
*Sacral Centre* Affirmation – 'I am creative and move with the flow of life'
*Root* Affirmation – 'I am fully supported by life. I give up my need for control'

## Emotional cause
Haemorrhoids in children can be an indication of emotional or physical abuse. The fear is of losing the abusive parent and yet wanting at the same time to push away. If there is a strong need to control you can be in a conflict because you want to release or reject something, yet your fear holds it in place.

## Reiki treatment
Treat the spleen with position **7** and then use position **22** to treat the problem directly.

## Recommended complementary treatment
• Eat high fibre foods.
• Avoid sugar and fat.
• Exercise to strengthen the abdominal muscles.
• Sitz baths with cypress oil and myrrh.

• Homoeopathy – Aesculus: for sharp burning pain; Arnica: for haemorrhoids that present after childbirth; Nux Vomica: for rectal itching; Sulphur: for a sore and bruised rectum. Consult a qualified homoeopathic practitioner.
• Bach flower therapy.

# HALITOSIS (BAD BREATH)

According to allopathic medicine, halitosis is related to poor oral hygiene. Infrequently it is caused by an underlying disease. Avoidance of foods like garlic and onion, and good dental practices, will help combat halitosis.

Natural healing methods state that bad breath is a symptom of an internal disorder. The source can be the gums, teeth, sinuses, lungs, stomach or the intestines. One of the most common causes of bad breath is constipation or generally poor elimination of waste due to inadequate fibre in the diet. Bad breath normally clears up on its own without treatment.

## Glands
Adrenals

## Chakras
*Solar Plexus* Affirmation – 'I release all anger and thoughts of revenge'
*Sacral Centre* Affirmation – 'I am an open and creative person. Life moves through me freely'

## Emotional cause
Halitosis represents deep fear and anger that has been suppressed so long it has backed up and become stale. What in your life can you forgive and release? Isn't it the time to open yourself to the majesty of creative expression and flow with the power of life?

**Reiki treatment**

Treat the liver, stomach and large intestines using positions **6** to **9**.

**Recommended complementary treatment**

• Eat several small meals a day so that the body can properly digest the food. Take drinks and soup between meals and not less than half-an-hour before eating or one hour afterwards. This is so the digestive juices will not be diluted.

• Lemon and lime will purify the breath.

• Drink purified water between meals to help with the removal of toxins from the body.

• Exercise helps in eliminating stored waste. Walking, jogging or running are all good.

• Supplements – beta-carotene, vitamins B complex, C and E. Caraway seeds are wonderful to chew and they aid in digestion and the breaking down of fats.

# HEPATITIS

According to modern allopathic medicine, hepatitis is an inflammation of the liver, which may result in the death of liver tissue. It is predominantly caused by viral infection but may be drug or toxin induced. There are several strains of the hepatitis virus: A, B, C, D and E. Hepatitis A and E are transmitted through contaminated food and water. Hepatitis B and C are transmitted sexually and through blood contact. Hepatitis B and C are particularly hazardous, as there is, as yet, no cure. People in high-risk occupations, such as health care professionals, should be immunised against Hepatitis B. It is important to consult a medical doctor for treatment of this disease. Initially, the symptoms of hepatitis appear as weakness, drowsiness, nausea, fever, headache, loss of appetite, aching muscles and malaise. There can also be tenderness in the area of the liver.

Natural healing methods indicate that hepatitis can be caused by a lifestyle that depresses the body's immunity. This can include poor diet, drug use, alcoholism and other unhealthy ways of living. The liver will be congested with fatty acids, which prevent blood from flowing freely through the organ. There can also be exposure to chemical toxins.

## Glands
Adrenals

## Chakras
*Solar Plexus* Affirmation – 'I embrace changes and I release all anger and resentment'

## Emotional cause
An infection in the liver indicates that we have stored emotions, primarily anger and resentment, in connection with our relationships. We are internally weakened because of a gathering of negative emotions. We may even feel helpless to change and are in a position to feel guilt and anger in these confronting situations.

## Reiki treatment
Use treatment positions **12**, **13** and **17** to treat the liver. You can also sandwich the liver area using one hand on the back over the right kidney and adrenal gland, and the other hand directly over the liver.

## Recommended complementary treatment
• Eat wholegrains, leafy, green vegetables and oats.
• Avoid alcohol, red meat, dairy products, poultry, eggs, sugar, oils, refined foods, spices and nuts.
• Consult a herbalist for the correct herbs to treat liver disease.

• Supplements – beta-carotene, folic acid, vitamins B, C and E.

# TOOTHACHE, TEETH AND GUM DISEASE

According to allopathic medicine toothache is experienced as a pain in a tooth or underlying gum, usually an early indication of tooth decay or dental abscess (collection of pus). Occasionally it is an indication of infected facial sinuses. The most common problem occurring in the gums is infection from poor dental hygiene. Good dental hygiene and regular dental visits can prevent most dental problems. Painkillers may be used during painful periods of toothache.

Natural healing methods indicate that tooth and gum disease is caused by a diet too high in animal protein, rich in fat and sugar, and devoid of fibre. Chinese medicine maintains that the liver nourishes the gums. The more the liver is stressed by toxins the greater the degeneration of the gums.

## Glands
Thyroid and adrenals

## Chakras
**Throat** Affirmation – 'I communicate my wisdom'
**Solar Plexus** Affirmation – 'I am strong and head my own inner wisdom'

## Emotional cause
Teeth are hard tissue and represent the core of our being. When we have a deep conflict about what we are saying the teeth and gums reflect this. Teeth also represent our wisdom. What inner wisdom are you not paying attention to? Is there something that you need to let go of so it will not become rotten?

## Reiki treatment

Treat the gums and teeth directly by laying your hands over the jaw-line. Also treat the liver using positions **6** to **8**.

## Recommended complementary treatment

• Eat raw fruits and vegetables, nuts, whole unrefined grains and green vegetables.
• Avoid meat, sugar, fizzy drinks, sweets, refined foods and overcooked foods.
• Massage gums with tea tree oil once a day.
• Brush teeth with baking soda to prevent pyorrhoea (gum disease) and to stop gingivitis.
• Use Chinese medicine to build up the liver.

# ULCERS (STOMACH OR PEPTIC)

According to allopathic medicine, peptic ulcers result from a breach in the lining of the stomach and oesophagus, which become infected by bacteria, usually experienced as a burning sensation in the abdomen. Pain passes with eating but recurs within a few hours. Rarely, bleeding ulcers cause blood-stained faeces and/or vomiting. This warrants immediate medical attention. Drugs that reduce acid levels in the stomach and drinking milk help ease symptoms of pain and burning, although ingesting milk if someone is lactose intolerant could cause discomfort.

Those who follow natural healing methods state that diet and lifestyle play central roles in the onset of ulcers. Salted, pickled and smoked foods are extremely hard to digest. Milk could be considered another factor, because many people are lactose intolerant. When they ingest milk products this will increase stomach discomfort. Stress in the workplace and at home are also factors.

## Glands
Adrenals

## Chakras
*Solar Plexus* Affirmation – 'I release what is eating at me mentally and emotionally'

## Emotional cause
Growing aggravation and irritation makes us bad tempered. It is usually our reaction to the event and not necessarily the event that is the cause. We end up with a short fuse and can easily explode, but also mull things over and over in our minds. When will you let go and let God in?

## Reiki treatment
Use treatment positions **6** and **7**.

## Recommended complementary treatment
• Eat four to six small meals a day, as it will put less stress on your stomach. Chew your food at least fifty times before swallowing.
• Eat protein and starch at separate meals; do not mix.
• See a nutritionist for a good diet that supports your stomach.
• Use meditation to relax. Try t'ai chi as a moving meditation to promote relaxation.
• Keep a journal to write out your deepest feelings.
• Bach flower therapy.
• Consult a homoeopathic practitioner.

# 6

# THE ENDOCRINE SYSTEM

The endocrine system of the body comprises glands and organs that contain endocrine cells. Endocrine cells produce chemical messengers (hormones) which are released into the bloodstream to control various functions of the body.

## ENDOCRINE GLANDS OF THE BODY

**Thyroid:** Located behind the windpipe (trachea), it regulates metabolism, growth and calcium levels.

**Pituitary:** Located within the brain, it stimulates growth, metabolism, milk production, adrenal and thyroid hormones, ovaries and testes, uterine contraction during labour and regulates urine production.

**Parathyroid:** Located behind the thyroid, it regulates calcium levels.

**Thymus:** Located behind the breastbone (sternum), it regulates the immune system.

**Pineal:** Located within the brain, it regulates biorhythms.

**Adrenals:** Located on the top of the kidneys, they regulate stress response, sodium and potassium excretion, growth, metabolism and sex drive.

## ORGANS CONTAINING ENDOCRINE CELLS

**Brain:** Responds to pain stimuli.

**Hypothalamus:** Located within the brain, it stimulates the pituitary gland.

**Kidneys:** Located near the base of the ribs, the kidneys regulate blood pressure, stimulate red blood cell production and control calcium and phosphorus production.

**Ovaries:** Located each side of the uterus, the ovaries stimulate female sexual development and regulate the female reproductive cycle.

**Pancreas:** Located beneath the stomach, the pancreas regulates blood glucose (sugar) levels and produces digestive enzymes.

**Placenta:** Located on the wall of the uterus during pregnancy, the placenta maintains conditions necessary for pregnancy.

**Stomach/Small Intestine:** Located below the liver, the stomach regulates digestion.

**Testes:** Responsible for genital, muscle and bone growth, the testes stimulate male sexual development.

Common conditions of the endocrine system dealt with in this section are diabetes mellitus, hypoglycaemia and thyroid disorders.

# DIABETES

According to modern allopathic medicine, diabetes mellitus results from an inability of the pancreas to maintain normal blood glucose levels. Insulin dependent diabetes mellitus (IDDM or Type 1) occurs when the pancreas produces little or no insulin. Non-insulin dependent diabetes mellitus (NIDDM or Type 2) occurs when the pancreas produces minimal insulin or cells are less receptive to the effects of insulin. Both conditions, if left untreated, can result in death. IDDM has been linked to a viral infection, which results in the destruction of insulin-producing cells. NIDDM is related to age and/or obesity. Treatment of IDDM is a balance between insulin injections, diet and exercise. NIDDM is treated with diet, exercise, in some cases medication to stimulate insulin production and, rarely, with insulin injections.

According to natural healing methods, high levels of stress, adrenal exhaustion and prolonged demands on the pancreas and liver cause diabetes. Diet is said to be a major contributory factor in this illness.

## Glands
Adrenals

## Chakras
*Solar Plexus* Affirmation – 'I release my need to control and allow life to flow freely through me'

## Emotional cause
Usually diabetes has to do with balancing the sweetness in our lives. We may not feel we deserve sweetness. It is only for others. Or we may feel that it is there for us, only we do not see it. A person with diabetes may lack the ability to love others, as well as the ability to love themselves.

## Reiki treatment
Treat the pancreas with position **6**, and the adrenals and kidneys with positions **12** and **13**.

## Recommended complementary treatment
• Eat wholegrains, vegetables (especially raw, green vegetables), pulses, whole and cooked fruit, Brussels sprouts, cucumbers, green beans, garlic, oatmeal, avocados and linseed oil.
• Avoid foods rich in fat, especially animal fat, dairy products, sugar, white flour and white rice.
• Avoid competitive sports and contact sports as diabetics may bruise more easily.
• Walk once a day for twenty to thirty minutes as exercise improves circulation.
• Use hydrotherapy – alternate hot and cold packs over the kidneys and pancreas to help insulin production and kidney waste elimination.

# HYPOGLYCAEMIA

According to allopathic medicine, hypoglycaemia results from an abnormally low blood glucose level. Commonly this occurs in people with diabetes when there is an alteration in the balance between diet, exercise and medication/insulin. Too much of one and not enough of the other will have a resultant impact on blood glucose levels. Rarely, it can result from excessive alcohol intake or insulin-producing tumours of the pancreas. Symptoms include: sweating, weakness, hunger, dizziness, trembling, headache, confusion, sometimes double vision and irrational behaviour. Eating foods containing sugar treats hypoglycaemia. If a person is unconscious then an injection of glucose or glucagon (hormone which counteracts insulin) is given. Persistent hypoglycaemia should be investigated by a medical practitioner.

Natural healing methods contend that hypoglycaemia often develops from the same dietary extremes as diabetes, but instead of a shortage of insulin excess insulin is produced. When there is too much insulin the pancreas is overworked and the result may be the onset of diabetes. This is often attributed to sugar abuse or an excess of animal protein.

## Glands
Adrenals

## Chakras
*Solar Plexus* Affirmation – 'I handle everything that life brings to me with ease'

## Emotional cause
Emotionally, hypoglycaemia points to the need to love yourself, to give to yourself first so that the love you are missing does not need to be replaced with sugar. There can be a sense of being overburdened by life. It is as if the sweetness in your life has gone and you look for something to replace it.

## Reiki treatment
Use positions **6** to **8** to treat the liver, pancreas and spleen. Then treat with positions **12** and **13** to treat the kidneys and adrenals.

## Recommended complementary treatment
• Eating a wide variety of food from the following list will help to strengthen the pancreas and regulate the blood sugar, and at the same time help to improve the fluid metabolism: grains and legumes, chlorophyll-rich foods, vegetables, fruits and herbs, and use licorice powder for a sweetener.
• Limit your intake of animal products to abalone, clams, cows' milk, yoghurt, lamb, kidneys, chicken or goose. You may also have small portions of fat-free beef.

• Avoid overuse of salt (as salt reduces blood sugar), fruit juices, sugar, excessive amounts of high protein foods, flour products, spices, dried fruit and refined carbohydrates.
• Vigorous exercises will lower blood sugar levels and reduce the need to produce insulin. Exercise will also improve the circulation.
• Look at how you are living life. Part of the healing and overcoming of the hypoglycaemic cycle involves being morally aware of how you live your life on the earth.

# THYROID DISORDERS (HYPOTHYROIDISM AND HYPERTHYROIDISM)

According to allopathic medicine, the thyroid is the endocrine gland responsible for regulating energy levels. Disturbances in thyroid function can occur as a result of infection, tumours, nutritional disorders, birth defects or surgical removal (thyroidectomy). Low thyroid activity (hypothyroidism) may result in tiredness, dry skin, hair loss, weight gain, constipation or cold sensitivity. High thyroid activity (hyperthyroidism) may produce fatigue, anxiety, sweating, palpitations, weight loss, diarrhoea or heat sensitivity. Medication is usually used to correct thyroid imbalance.

Those who follow natural healing methods contend that a balanced diet is better than taking synthetic thyroid hormones. It is important also to support your health by taking adequate exercise.

**Glands**
Thyroid

## Chakras
*Throat* Affirmation – 'I trust in my willingness to live in harmony'

## Emotional cause
The thyroid gland is responsible for, among other things, the regulation of the breathing process. It is also connected to the coming of life in a physical form. It is our desire to live and commit ourselves to entering into life. If that commitment is weak then the message to the thyroid will be confused. Do I sustain life or not? Hyperthyroidism is a stressful response and one that mirrors a self-centred personality. It can also indicate a feeling of choking on life. Hypothyroidism can mirror a personality that feels hopeless and defeated. We have little desire to enter into anything; what is the use?

## Reiki treatment
Treat the thyroid using position **4** or **4a**.

## Recommended complementary treatment
• Eat foods rich in iodine such as seaweed, raw foods, unrefined wholefoods, wholegrains, vegetables, sprouted seeds and beans, garlic and radishes.
• Homoeopathy – Belladonna: for flushed face and staring eyes; Lycopus: for bulging eyes; Iodium: feeling obsessive and unable to stop hurrying. Consult a qualified homoeopathic practitioner.
• Do yoga exercises that are specific to the throat.

# 7
# THE
# INTEGUMENTARY
# SYSTEM

**The integumentary system** comprises the skin and its derivatives such as hair, nails, glands and nerve endings. Each has a vital role to play in the overall protection and healthy functioning of the human body.

The skin is the body's largest organ. Its functions are:

(1) to aid in temperature regulation
(2) to protect the internal organs from injury, disease, dehydration and ultraviolet (UV) radiation
(3) to receive and transmit information about touch, temperature, pressure and pain
(4) to remove heat, water and excessive chemicals/waste products
(5) to aid the immune response by assisting the blood flow and
(6) to begin the production of vitamin D.

Hair on the scalp and body also helps to regulate the temperature and protect from UV radiation. Eyelashes, eyebrows, and nasal and external ear canal hair help to protect the body from invading foreign bodies such as insects and dust. Touch receptors in the skin are activated when hair is moved, even if only slightly.

Three glands are located within the skin: sebaceous (oil) glands; sudoriferous (sweat) glands; and, within the external ear canal, a modified sweat gland called a ceruminous gland. Sebaceous glands secrete an oily substance called sebum. Sebum helps to control excessive evaporation of water from the skin. The oily substance also keeps the skin soft and pliable, and prevents the growth of some bacteria. Sudoriferous glands help in temperature regulation by emptying their watery contents on to the skin, which evaporate to cool the skin. Small amounts of excessive chemical and waste products also leave the body during this process. Ceruminous glands secrete a wax-like substance into the external ear canal creating a sticky surface and preventing foreign bodies like dust and insects from entering the inner ear.

Nerve endings located in the skin detect changes in skin temperature, pressure, touch and pain. These signals are relayed to the brain, which in turn sends a signal to the body to react to the changes.

Common ailments of the integumentary system dealt with in this section are abrasions, acne, body odour, burns, cold sores, dandruff, eczema, fungal skin infections, hair loss, hives and nettle rash, insect bites, itching, nail problems, psoriasis, rashes, urticaria and warts.

# ABRASIONS, CUTS AND WOUNDS

According to allopathic medicine, a wound results from damage to skin/mucous membranes, which may also involve underlying tissue. Closed wounds do not breach the skin/mucous membrane surface, whereas open wounds do. Wounds are classified as:

(1) incisional, clean-cut
(2) abrasion, scraping
(3) laceration, torn or ripped
(4) penetrating, foreign object remains in wound

All wounds should be rinsed to remove foreign particles such as dirt, then cleaned with an antiseptic, and a clean or sterile dressing applied. When there are deep wounds or prolonged bleeding, stitches may be needed. With penetrating injuries, foreign objects should not be removed until reviewed by a medical practitioner.

According to natural healing methods, trauma and damage to the tissues cause abrasions and wounds. All cuts need to be cleaned thoroughly. Wounds need to be placed in ice water immediately to stop the bleeding and reduce the chances of inflammation. The area needs to be kept clean and bandaged.

### Glands
Depends on where the abrasion or wound is located

### Chakras
Depends on where the abrasion or wound is located

### Emotional cause
Is your abrasion or wound located on the left or right side of your body? Is it located on a certain part of your body? The left side of the body is the receiving side and the right side is the giving side. If you are prone to hurt one particular side or part of your body more than the other this might be telling you something, since often we hurt ourselves on an energetically weakened area. Ask what this abrasion or wound is telling you. For example, if you keep wounding your knees it may point to the need for humility and asking for help; while

the right side of your body could indicate an unwillingness to give out of yourself, for whatever reason.

## Reiki treatment
If you are working with trauma on an arm or leg, place your hands in a sandwich fashion with one hand on top and the other hand below. For other areas place your hands down over the bandaged area gently.

## Recommended complementary treatment
• Homoeopathy – Arnica.
• For topical application to the abrasion or wound use aloe vera juice, tea tree oil, vitamin E cream or arnica cream.
• Bach flower therapy.

# ACNE

According to modern allopathic medicine, acne is an acute infection of the sebaceous glands within the skin. Onset generally occurs during puberty although it can also occur in older people when there is an increase in the production of sebum. This is thought to be related to the upsurge in hormonal activity at this time. Acne usually appears on the face, upper back and shoulders. In severe cases of acne, scarring can occur as small sacs of tissue destroy and replace normal skin cells. Although it is speculated that diet may play a role in the development of acne, there is no definitive correlation. Allopathic treatment of acne usually includes skin cleansers, topical ointments, antibiotics (in severe cases) and ultraviolet light. Drugs which increase sebum production, such as steroids and male/female hormones, are often avoided.

From a natural healing perspective, acne is the result of over-acidic blood caused by too much refined food, an excessive amount of dairy products, foods high in fat and cholesterol, sugar, chocolate and other foods with a high sugar content. These are the foods that teenagers seem to crave. Natural healing methods maintain that a diet of unprocessed wholegrains, vegetables, beans and fish, with very limited amounts of animal products will lead to clearer skin.

## Glands
Pituitary, thalamus, thyroid, parathyroid, thymus, adrenals and gonads

## Chakras
*Third Eye* Affirmation – 'I use my intuition and my ability to see clearly'
*Throat* Affirmation – 'I trust the process and communicate my desires'
*Solar Plexus* Affirmation – 'I am discovering who I am and what is my reality'
*Sacral Centre* Affirmation – 'I acknowledge the sexual side of who I am becoming'

## Emotional cause
Puberty is the time for a declaration of independence from our parents and a desire to establish who we are. There is great emotional upheaval and accompanying feelings of discomfort about our changing bodies and increased sexual urges. We are pushing away our support system and yet have not fully developed our own legs to stand on. Our unrest is usually accompanied by anger at life, parents and self. The liver is the organ that holds unexpressed anger, and what is not expressed may cause the skin to erupt. We are then in a vicious circle of not liking our appearance and this distress may further aggravate the condition.

## Reiki treatment

When working over inflamed areas on the skin it is always best to place a clean sterile gauze pad directly on the area to be treated before touching the area. Work on the affected areas, kidneys, liver and reproductive areas. Treat using positions **1**, **4** to **9**, and **29**.

## Recommended complementary treatment

• Homoeopathy – Sulphur: for long-standing acne; Calcarea Sulphur: for blind pimples; Hepar Sulphur: for large pimples that look like boils. Consult a qualified homoeopathic practitioner.

• Use meditation – usually ten to fifteen minutes twice a day.

• Use creative visualisation to see yourself as being on your own feet and happily moving forward to your goals.

• T'ai chi movements will harmonise the body and quieten the mind.

• Dance and movement will reduce any stress that has built up.

• Swimming and water sports will help get anger and stress out of the body.

• Attend youth groups where, through talking, singing and team activities a sense of community is established and upheld.

• Bach flower therapy.

# BODY ODOUR

According to modern allopathic medicine, body odour is an unpleasant smell caused by decomposing skin bacteria. As the body sweats it releases water and other chemicals on to the skin, providing an ideal environment for the growth of bacteria, especially around the genitals and armpits where proteins and fatty acids are released by specialised sweat glands. Some people have over-active sweat glands. Body odour also occurs from eating garlic, curry and other spicy foods. Bathing daily and the use of a deodorant can prevent body odour.

Those who follow natural healing methods see the skin as a major organ of elimination, excreting toxins from the kidneys, liver, lymph and blood. When the blood-cleansing abilities of these organs are hampered by a diet that is rich in animal foods and sugar the problem of odour persists. Odour occurs because many of these products decay rapidly inside the body.

## Glands
Lymph, adrenals and gonads

## Chakras
*Solar Plexus* Affirmation – 'I am defining myself by what I take into my body and hold on to'
*Sacral Centre* Affirmation – 'I am deserving of a clean atmosphere to experience my sexuality'
*Root* Affirmation – 'At the root of everything is my stability and thoughts of myself'

## Emotional cause
When I first went to Eastern Europe I recognised the smell of fear permeating the skin of all the people just free from communism. They had also lost sight of themselves as valuable people. As they have changed, their bodies and hygiene have also changed. Repression breeds fear and lack of concern about the self and others.

## Reiki treatment
Use positions **12** and **13** to support the liver; **19** and **20** for the lymph glands.

## Recommended complementary treatment
• Avoid eating animal fats, red meats, dairy products, hydrogenated fats and sugar.
• Avoid anti-perspirants. They contain aluminium and prevent the body from eliminating waste in a normal and healthy manner through the perspiration.
• Hydrotherapy – use a loofah sponge to brush the skin thoroughly while showering to help eliminate waste more rapidly.
• Epsom salts baths can help with body odour from either external or internal causes. Dissolve 1 to $1^1/_2$ lb Epsom salts in a hot bath and soak for fifteen minutes. Finish with a cold shower. Use once a day for a week then reduce to two to three times a week until the body odour returns to normal.
• Use zinc, chlorophyll or essential fatty acids supplements to purify the blood.

# BURNS

Both practitioners of modern allopathic medicine and natural healing methods describe burns as resulting from the skin and/or mucous membranes (lining of the respiratory system) being subjected to excessive heat, toxic chemicals, radiation or electricity. They are classified according to the extent of tissue injury involved. First-degree burns involve the top layer of skin which becomes red, swollen and tender. Second-degree burns involve deeper layers of the skin causing blistering. Third-degree burns involve the full thickness of the skin and in some cases muscle tissue as well.

Cold running water should be immediately applied. Material that is stuck to the affected area should not be removed. Cover burns with clean/sterile non-stick material. Do not apply creams, lotions or ointments unless advised by a physician. Where chemicals and electricity are involved exercise caution. Dilute chemicals with plenty of water and turn off electricity source (if safe) before assisting the victim. Reiki will help to encourage healing of all degrees of burns.

## Glands
Depends on where the burn or burns are located

## Chakras
Depends on where the burn or burns are located

## Emotional cause
The underlying emotional cause of burns may be that one is burning up with anger and is incensed both mentally and emotionally. Attention needs to be paid to what side and what part of the body are burned as this can indicate further underlying emotional causes (see also 'Emotional cause' for section on Abrasions, Cuts and Wounds). For example, a burn on the foot may indicate a burning pain about a move or decision we have taken about our security that has triggered an emotional response.

## Reiki treatment
It is important never to place the hand directly on the burn. Treat above, below and to each side of the burn, to encourage healing of the skin. Cover the area with a sterile gauze pad. Often the pain will increase if you work too closely to the actual burned area, so keep your hand far enough away from the skin.

## Recommended complementary treatment
• Apply the gelatinous inner contents of aloe vera leaves to a minor burn. The combination of propolis and aloe gel soothes and has an anti-inflammatory and antibiotic effect.
• Homoeopathy – Arnica: used internally for shock;

Causticum: taken internally to reduce pain in severe cases where there is restlessness and blister formation; Calendula lotion or Hypericum lotion applied externally. Consult a qualified homoeopathic practitioner.
• Hydrotherapy – to prevent blister formation immerse the area in cold water immediately until there is no pain. For transfer to hospital wrap the area in wet towels and keep moist.
• Chinese medicine – apply carrot juice or cucumber juice externally.
• Supplements – apply vitamin E oil after soaking in water.
• Bach flower therapy – take four drops of Rescue Remedy. Also you can apply Rescue Cream on the burn.

# COLD SORES

According to allopathic medicine, a cold sore is a blister appearing in, or around, the mouth, usually caused by the herpes simplex type 1 (HSV1) virus. Initial exposure to the HSV1 virus may go unnoticed, but symptoms of influenza may be experienced. The virus remains dormant within the nerve cells until stress, exposure to heat/wind, common colds or infection activate the virus causing cold sores to appear. Symptoms can be treated with anti-viral medication if painful.

Those who follow natural healing methods consider that the true cause of cold sores is an imbalance in the spleen, liver and stomach, usually brought on by eating a diet rich in acidic foods and spices. Eating acidic foods has been found to weaken the immune system. Once the immune system is depressed, the virus can take hold. Stress also plays a role in the onset of this condition.

## Glands
Adrenals

## Chakras
*Solar Plexus* Affirmation – 'I release all the stress that I have been holding on to'

## Emotional cause
The mouth acts as a gateway where we take in things to assimilate. Cold sores can be showing us that what we have taken in has caused us to react with irritation. The mouth is also where we express ourselves, so conflict could be occurring here as a result of non-communication as our words are festering in our mouths.

## Reiki treatment
Use positions **6** to **7** and **12** and **13** to strengthen the liver and kidneys. You can also do Reiki directly on the cold sore, but cover with a sterile gauze pad first.

## Recommended complementary treatment
• Avoid eating red meat, high protein foods, spices and tomatoes.
• Liver detoxification – do a one-to-three-day carrot juice fast to cleanse the liver (see p. 59).
• Apply ice at the first sign of tingling for fifteen to twenty minutes. Afterwards apply vitamin E cream. Do this three to four times daily.

# DANDRUFF

According to allopathic medicine, dandruff is the shedding of dead skin from the scalp, face, chest and back. It is usually caused by dermatitis. If anti-dandruff shampoo does not soothe the itchy, flaking area then corticosteroids and anti-fungal medications may be prescribed.

For those who follow natural healing methods, dandruff is the body's way of eliminating the excess proteins and fats which cannot be assimilated by the body. It is thought that dandruff is the result of an imbalance in the liver and/or kidneys. Also, a diet high in acidic foods can produce dandruff.

## Glands
Pineal, hypothalamus and adrenals

## Chakras
*Crown* Affirmation – 'I am open to support from higher sources'
*Solar Plexus* Affirmation – 'I release all things that are irritating to me'
*Sacral Centre* Affirmation – 'I accept both sides of my nature as natural and spontaneous'

## Emotional cause
The condition of dandruff indicates a need to release excess mental energy. Thoughts that are obsolete need to fall away from you. Hard thinking, ingrained attitudes and thought patterns that no longer support you also need to be eliminated.

## Reiki treatment
Use position **7** to support the liver, positions **12** and **13** to support the kidneys, and position **2** on the head.

## Recommended complementary treatment
• Follow an alkalising diet that consists of low-fat animal products, such as white fish, raw vegetable juices and cooked

vegetables. Eat wholegrains, salads, tofu, seeds such as sunflower and pumpkin, and seaweed.
• Avoid eating foods rich in saturated fats, red meat, eggs and dairy products, citrus, sugar and alcohol.
• Physiotherapy – scalp massage using a mixture of pure distilled water, twenty drops of grain alcohol and a few drops of pine oil; massage into scalp and rinse well. Rosemary hair rinse will stimulate and clear the scalp.
• Walking, jogging, cycling or any type of aerobic exercise that is done regularly will stimulate the circulation to clear skin problems including dandruff.

# ECZEMA

According to allopathic medicine, eczema is a form of dermatitis that causes the skin to become red, inflamed, itchy, scaly and blistered. The cause is unknown; however, there is a hereditary link in people predisposed to allergies. Eczema can occur anywhere on the skin. It is treated with soothing ointments and occasionally corticosteroids. Fabrics such as wool, silk and synthetics should be avoided.

According to natural healing methods, impaired kidney and liver function can cause eczema. Also, a diet rich in saturated fats has been known to cause this problem.

## Glands
Adrenals

## Chakras
**Solar Plexus** Affirmation – 'I release all toxic thinking and feelings'
**Sacral Centre** Affirmation – 'I am in harmony with my sexuality'

## Emotional cause

Eczema is an indication that we need to release something, such as an old thought pattern, so that something new may come in. It can also indicate that we may feel blocked and interfered with. Eczema can also indicate that we are uncomfortable with our image and ourselves.

## Reiki treatment

Treat the liver with positions **6** and **7**, the kidneys with positions **12** and **13**, and work directly on gauze covered areas where eczema is present.

## Recommended complementary treatment

• Herbs to cleanse the blood include dandelion root, goldenseal or chaparral leaves.
• Chinese medicine to improve the energy in the kidneys and liver.
• A four-to-five-day vegetable juice fast will clear the body of toxins.

# FUNGAL SKIN INFECTIONS

According to modern allopathic medicine, fungal infections are caused by the growth of fungi (mould, mildew and yeast) on the body. The most common superficial infections are candidiasis, caused by the yeast *Candida albicans*, and tinea (ringworm and athlete's foot). Fungi thrive in warm, moist environments so affected areas should be kept clean and dry. Anti-fungal medications may be prescribed. Clothes should also be changed frequently.

Natural healing methods state that the problem lies within the framework of a suppressed or impaired immune system. The immune system may have been weakened due to accumulated toxins that exist in the lymph, liver, intestines and spleen. All natural treatment is designed to cleanse and increase the strength of the immune system.

## Glands
Thymus and adrenals

## Chakras
*Heart* Affirmation – 'I open to love and forgiveness. I let go of past reaction'
*Solar Plexus* Affirmation – 'I release the past and am strong in my present moment'

## Emotional cause
What is stagnating in your belief system? Usually fungal infections indicate a refusal to let go of the past and move forward into a brighter future. Are you allowing the past to rule you?

## Reiki treatment
Treat the liver, spleen and intestines with positions **6** to **8**. Also use position **18** to strengthen the immune system.

## Recommended complementary treatment
• Eat chlorophyll-rich foods and seaweed.
• Avoid consuming excess salt.
• Use meditation to calm the mind and enable you to release past emotional reactions.
• Use herbal preparations to cleanse the system.
• Bach flower therapy.

# HAIR LOSS

According to allopathic medicine, a minimal amount of hair loss each day is normal. Excessive hair loss may be an indication of poor diet, excessive shampooing, frequent combing or blow-drying. Fungal infections may also cause increased hair loss. Partial or full baldness is hereditarily linked. Rarely it may be an indication of decreased thyroid activity. There is no effective allopathic treatment for hair loss.

Those who follow natural healing methods see hair loss as being a direct reflection of the condition of the blood and the blood cleansing organs, especially the kidneys, the adrenals and the sex organs. The more toxicity in the blood the poorer the condition of the hair follicles, which nourish the hair and support its growth. Prolonged and chronic stress can affect the adrenal glands and cause hair loss.

## Glands
Pineal, hypothalamus and adrenals

## Chakras
*Crown* Affirmation – 'I release my need to control and am supported by life'
*Solar Plexus* Affirmation – 'I trust the process of life. I release all fear and tension'

## Emotional cause
Perhaps you do not trust the process of life. Your hair represents your freedom, strength and power. If you are experiencing hair loss, what part of your own strength and power have you lost? What do you really want to do, regardless of what others may want? It is a sign to be true to yourself. Let go of fear, stress and tension in your life and be who you wish to be.

## Reiki treatment
Use positions 2, 7 and 8, 12 and 13 to work with the head, liver, spleen and pancreas.

## Recommended complementary treatment

• Consult a nutritionist or a herbalist to design a diet to support the kidneys, spleen and pancreas, and cleanse the blood.
• Bach flower therapy.

# HIVES AND NETTLE RASH
## (URTICARIA)

According to allopathic medicine, urticaria is an inflammation of the skin characterised by white/yellow raised lumps and itching. During an allergic reaction histamine is released from skin cells causing fluid to leak from surface blood vessels into surrounding skin tissue. Urticaria is an indication of an allergy to food, food additives or drugs. Treatment includes soothing lotions and antihistamines.

Natural healing methods state that hives are the body's way of eliminating toxins that have built up in the liver, kidneys, large intestine, bloodstream and lymph system. When all these systems are so overburdened the only way of eliminating toxicity is through the skin.

### Glands
Adrenals

### Chakras
*Solar Plexus* Affirmation – 'I open and release all toxic thoughts and feelings'

### Emotional cause
Hives are thought to indicate that something has got under our skin. We are frustrated and will not let go of the demand: it must be this way and no other. When we itch it can be the result of feeling helpless, and this is made worse by our tension and stress.

## Reiki treatment
Use positions **6** to **8** to work with the liver and large intestines. Use positions **12** and **13** to work with the kidneys. Also use position **18** to stimulate the immune system.

## Recommended complementary treatment
• Hydrotherapy draws the toxins from the skin. Dissolve 1 lb baking soda in a hot bath and sit there for at least half-an-hour.
• Use thirty drops echinacea tincture topically four to five times a day.
• Follow a carrot juice fast for three days to eliminate toxins (see p. 59).
• Bach flower therapy.

# INSECT BITES

According to allopathic medicine, insects puncture the skin to feed off tiny surface blood vessels. An allergic reaction is activated as the insect's saliva and faeces enter the puncture site. This can cause mild to severe reactions, including redness, swelling, rash and pimples. Usually insect bites are of little problem other than being annoying. However, in tropical areas insects like the mosquito carry diseases such as malaria. To treat insect bites clean the affected area and apply a soothing cream. In severe cases antihistamines may be prescribed.

Natural healing methods can be used for those who develop a normal irritation or reaction to an insect bite. These normally subside after forty-eight hours. See a physician if you suffer an allergic reaction to an insect bite.

## Glands
Adrenals

### Chakras
*Solar Plexus* Affirmation – 'I open and release all toxic thoughts and feelings'

### Emotional cause
Insect bites are thought to indicate that something has got under our skin, as with hives. We find we are frustrated and will not let go of the demand: it must be this way and no other. When we itch it can be the result of feeling helpless, and this is made worse by tension and stress. Also, it is important to see which side of the body the bite is on. Does the bite become a source of irritation or an external manifestation of an internal frustration?

### Reiki treatment
Use positions **6** to **8** to work with the liver and large intestines. Use positions **12** and **13** to work with the kidneys. Also use position **18** to stimulate the immune system.

### Recommended complementary treatment
• Hydrotherapy draws the toxins from the skin. Dissolve 1 lb baking soda in a hot bath and sit there for at least half-an-hour.
• Use thirty drops echinacea tincture topically four to five times a day.
• Bach flower therapy.

# ITCHING

Allopathic medicine states that itching is an intense tingling or ticklish sensation. It may be localised (in one site) or generalised (all over). The cause of itching is not known. However, it is usually an indication of an underlying problem or allergic reaction. Localised itching may indicate fungal infections, insect bites, lice or scabies. Generalised itching may indicate systemic problems such as eczema, chicken pox, measles and kidney disease. Treatment varies and includes soothing lotions and moisturisers. In severe cases anti-histamines and corticosteroids are prescribed.

According to natural healing methods, itching occurs when the body is attempting to discharge waste products that the kidneys and liver have not been able to remove from the blood. The skin is an eliminating organ and will attempt to rid the body of toxins when the kidneys and liver become sluggish and overworked.

## Glands
Adrenals

## Chakras
*Solar Plexus* Affirmation – 'I release all toxic thinking and feeling from my body and mind'

## Emotional cause
Itching is an irritation that is affecting our whole body, our whole being. What or who is irritating us so badly? What do we want to run from or to scratch away from us? It can also be that someone is irritated with us and we are being over-sensitive.

## Reiki treatment
Treat the kidneys with positions **12** and **13**. Treat the liver with positions **6** and **7**.

## Recommended complementary treatment
• Use thirty drops echinacea tincture topically four to five times a day.
• Follow a carrot juice fast for three days to eliminate toxins (see p. 59).
• Bach flower therapy.

# NAIL PROBLEMS

According to modern allopathic medicine, nail problems occur as a result of trauma or infection. Anti-fungal medications or soothing lotions may be prescribed.

Those who follow natural healing methods consider that nail problems can reflect different health issues. The state of the nail can be an indicator of health issues you may be dealing with. Look at the list below to see some common comparisons.

*White half moons* can indicate excess sugar consumption and a calcium deficiency.

*Ridges in the nails* can indicate a protein or vitamin A deficiency and consumption of excess salt.

*Pale beds for the nails* can indicate anaemia.

*Peeling nails* can indicate a vitamin A deficiency.

*Poor nail growth* indicates a zinc deficiency.

*Splitting nails* indicate acidic blood and mineral deficiency, plus excess intake of sugary and refined foods.

*Spoon-shaped nails* can indicate excess consumption of refined foods and minerals deficiency.

*Thin, brittle nails* indicate a deficiency of iron, calcium and vitamin D.

## Glands
Adrenals

## Chakras
*Solar Plexus* Affirmation – 'I take in all that is necessary to support me to live fully'

## Emotional cause
Nails represent our inner core. They also represent our spiri-

tual energy. The nails are often affected when we are going through high levels of change or having a hard time dealing with the changes. They can also represent aggression.

## Reiki treatment

Treat the liver, spleen and pancreas with positions **6** and **7**. Also treat the kidneys using positions **12** and **13**.

## Recommended complementary treatment

• Eat foods that will strengthen the liver such as dark green, leafy vegetables, grains, beans, seaweed and sprouts.
• Avoid drinking coffee, tea and alcohol.
• Use Bach flower Rescue Cream on the cuticles.
• Take vitamin and mineral supplements.

# PSORIASIS AND RASHES

According to allopathic medicine, a rash is the major manifestation of psoriasis, and also of many immune response conditions. A rash is a response to any invading organism, foreign or domestic, i.e. from within the body (in which case this is an auto-immune response) or from outside the body (i.e. an immune response). Psoriasis is a disorder of auto-immunity.

With psoriasis there is abnormal growth of the skin cells. New cells become thickened and covered with dead cells, resulting in red, inflamed, scaly, flaky skin. The cause is unknown but there is a heredity factory. Attacks of psoriasis are related to emotional stress, physical illness and skin damage. It may be accompanied by arthritis-like symptoms or joint pain and stiffness. Treatment includes exposure to sunlight or ultraviolet light and moisturising creams. Severe cases may be prescribed corticosteroids and other medication.

A rash is characterised by localised (in one site) and

generalised (all over) red, inflamed skin, which may blister or form pustules (pus-filled blisters), or small, raised lumps or nodules. Rashes may also be accompanied by a fever, indicating an infectious disease like chicken pox or measles. Rashes also occur during fungal infections and where there is kidney disease. Rashes are also characteristic of eczema and tinea. Treatment includes soothing lotions and occasionally anti-histamines.

All skin eruptions and rashes are seen by those who follow natural healing methods as the body's way of eliminating waste that is not being properly filtered by the kidneys, liver and spleen. In some cases toxins are being reintroduced into the bloodstream and lymph system from the wall of the large intestine. Sensitivity to certain foods can also cause this condition.

## Glands
Adrenals

## Chakras
*Solar Plexus* Affirmation – 'I release all toxic thinking and emotions from my body. I am strong within myself'

## Emotional cause
Psoriasis and rashes indicate a build-up of mental stress that is triggered by poor health or a lack of resistance. What emotional patterns have you not released that are holding you back? Do you have some issues that are long dead and need to be let go?

## Reiki treatment
Treat the kidneys, liver and spleen using positions **6**, **7**, **12** and **13**. Work over the affected area after covering with a sterile gauze dressing.

## Recommended complementary treatment
• Meditate on what needs to be released from your mind.
• Write a journal about your emotions and what has got under your skin.
• Have herbal treatments from a qualified therapist.
• Swim in the ocean as the salt water is excellent treatment for the skin.
• Use Chinese medicine to strengthen the liver and kidneys.
• Consult a qualified homoeopathic practitioner.
• Bach flower therapy.

# WARTS

According to allopathic medicine, warts are an abnormal growth of the top layer of skin caused by the human papilloma virus (HPV). They are classified according to their location, e.g. hands, feet, genitals. Generally treatment is not necessary. However, occasionally they are treated using medication, cryosurgery (freezing), electrocautery (burning), laser therapy and curettage (scraping).

Those who follow natural healing methods view warts as a viral infection and a sign that the immune system has been weakened. Immediate repair of the immune system must begin.

## Glands
Thymus, adrenals and gonads

## Chakras
**Heart** Affirmation – 'I am able to freely give and receive love'
**Solar Plexus** Affirmation – 'I am nourished by life'
**Sacral Centre** Affirmation – 'I am in perfect harmony and peace'
**Root** Affirmation – 'I am strong, healthy and flexible'

## Emotional cause

Warts are seen as a mental stagnation that indicates dislike of the self. You are unable to see your own beauty. Perhaps you have not forgiven yourself for something in your past and may think of yourself as ugly as a result.

## Reiki treatment

Place your hand down on the wart after covering with a sterile cloth. Also treat the immune system using position **18**.

## Recommended complementary treatment

• Apply vitamin E cream directly to the wart. Or apply Vitamin A oil directly to the wart three times a day. Cover with sterile gauze.
• Supplements – beta-carotene, vitamins B1, B6, C and E, and zinc.
• Consult a qualified homoeopathic practitioner.

# 8

# THE LYMPHATIC AND
# IMMUNE SYSTEMS

**The lymphatic system** of the body comprises organs, tissues and ducts that transport lymph (a milky fluid made up of white blood cells, proteins and fat) around the body and drains into the bloodstream. It forms part of the immune system. The major function of the lymphatic system is to aid in the fight against infection and cancer. Lymph fluid surrounding cells returns to the heart through lymphatic vessels. Within these vessels are filters, or lymph nodes, which filter out bacteria, viruses and foreign bodies. The nodes contain white blood cells that react to neutralise invading particles. Lymph nodes and lymph vessels become swollen and tender when an infection is present in surrounding organs and tissue.

The immune system is made up of the various cells and proteins that are responsible for protecting the body from harmful bacteria, viruses and foreign bodies. There are essentially two components to the immune system: the innate immune system and the adaptive immune system.

## THE INNATE IMMUNE SYSTEM

**The eyes, mouth, nose,** airways, stomach and intestines, vagina, urethra and skin all provide a physical barrier to prevent the invasion of bacteria, viruses and foreign bodies. Reflexes such as coughing and sneezing help to keep

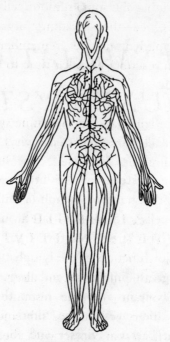

*The lymphatic system*

invading particles from entering the body through the nose and mouth. Naturally occurring bacteria in the stomach, intestine and urethra inhibit the growth of foreign organisms. Chemicals in tears and the mouth help destroy invading bacteria. Acid levels in the stomach and intestine also inhibit bacterial growth.

# THE ADAPTIVE IMMUNE
# SYSTEM

**While the innate immune** system acts to prevent invasion of harmful organisms, the adaptive immune system targets specific bacteria, viruses, fungi or tumour cells. Specialised white blood cells called lymphocytes are vital in the function of the immune system. Lymphocytes recognise invading viruses, bacteria, fungi and some tumour cells, and then act to destroy them. Once the invading organism has been destroyed, surviving lymphocytes 'remember' the responsible organism and can react before it has time to have any adverse effect on the body.

Conditions of the lymphatic and immune systems dealt with in this section are allergies (hypersensitivity), fever, immuno-deficiency/auto-immune disorders, swollen glands and tonsillitis.

# ALLERGIES (HYPERSENSITIVITY)

According to allopathic medicine, an allergy is a condition in which an inappropriate immune response is triggered by contact with an otherwise harmless substance. Allergic reactions often result from skin contact with chemicals, inhalation of dust, pollen or other airborne particles, and ingestion of particular foods. Reactions range from mild to severe and, in rare cases, if untreated, death. Treatment options include avoidance of the allergen, medication to treat the symptoms, and desensitisation.

Natural healing methods state that allergies often arise when the liver is unable to neutralise certain substances that build up within the body and then trigger an immune reaction. The substance that the body recognises as foreign is called an antigen. Antigens accumulate in the body in such places as the lymph system, intestines, liver and spleen. The body's immune system constantly works overtime to rid the body of this antigen, which, in turn, can cause a breakdown of the immune system, making the person even more sensitive to the substances.

Diet can also be a factor for many people with allergies.

Refined sugar, wheat, vinegar and milk products can trigger an allergy. Try removing these substances from your diet and follow a cleansing diet of high fibre and vegetables to restore good body chemistry. Slowly reintroduce these substances one by one. At the first sign of recurring allergy the substance is withdrawn. You should only undertake a cleansing diet like this under the supervision of a nutritionist or medical practitioner.

## Glands
Pituitary, thalamus, thyroid, parathyroid, thymus, adrenals and gonads

## Chakras
*Third Eye* Affirmation – 'I open my intuition and see clearly'
*Throat* Affirmation – I trust the process as it unfolds for me'
*Heart* Affirmation – 'I give unconditional love to myself'
*Solar Plexus* Affirmation – 'I embrace who I am and what is my reality'
*Sacral Centre* Affirmation – 'I am open to the sexual side of who I am or am becoming'

## Emotional cause
Allergies seem to be brought on or made worse by stress, both real and imagined. With respiratory problems associated with allergies, such as asthma, a reaction could be caused by a feeling of being smothered by love, so that there is not enough room to breathe. When people feel isolated and cut off from their families and peer group (as an outsider looking in), their thinking is toxic and the skin will erupt in a rash. It can also be thought of as a denial of their power.

## Reiki treatment

Using hand positions **1**, **4** to **8**, and **18**. Treat the sinuses, throat, lungs, liver, spleen, stomach and intestines. Spend time working on the skin if there is a rash. Drink 1 to 1½ litres of good water a day to help flush the system.

## Recommended complementary treatment

• Homoeopathy – Allium cepa: for the relief of runny nose and burning watery eyes. Consult a qualified homoeopathic practitioner.
• Daily aerobic exercise will help to cleanse the body of antigens through the sweat glands.
• Use ginger compresses on the liver to eliminate accumulated toxins.
• Meditate on positive thoughts and images.
• Keep a journal listing all self-criticism you indulge in on a daily basis. Substitute a positive thought for each negative one.
• Singing helps to strengthen the spleen – the key allergy-fighting organ.
• Bach flower therapy.

# FEVER

According to modern allopathic medicine, fever is defined as a body temperature greater than 37 to 37.5°C. Shivering, headache, sweating, thirst, increased breathing and reddened skin may also be experienced. In extreme cases confusion, fits and coma may occur if untreated. A fever is the body's response to infection. Fevers in children under six, high fevers and those accompanied by extreme symptoms should always be referred to a physician immediately. Otherwise treat with cool cloths, fans, loose clothing, aspirin (adults only) or paracetamol. Note: Do not take aspirin if you have been advised NOT to because of another problem.

According to natural healing methods, a fever is the body's way of curing an underlying problem. Therefore it should not be repressed unless the temperature rises above 37°C. Take plenty of liquids to keep the body hydrated; this can be in the form of water or diluted fruit juices. Stay warm and rest as much as possible. Avoid foods until the fever has broken, then only eat light foods that are easily digested.

## Glands
Pineal, thymus and adrenals

## Chakras
*Crown* Affirmation – 'I open myself to receive support and love from higher sources'
*Heart* Affirmation – 'I stay centred and loving in this process of healing'
*Solar Plexus* Affirmation – 'I support my healing processes and allow what is harmful to be released'

## Emotional cause
Fever can be a way of burning off negative thought forms (or negative self-talk) that have been held on to. It can relate to inner conflict and something that is really burning us up. We may have intense anger or some other hot emotion coming to the surface for us to look at and heal.

## Reiki treatment
Use the immune system stimulation position number **18** (treating others) to prevent shock in the case of high fevers. Basically support all toxin-eliminating organs using positions **6** to **8**.

## Recommended complementary treatment

• Avoid eating dairy products as they create mucus, animal products, and wheat products, such as flour, pasta and bread.
• Homoeopathy – Aconite: for sudden onset of fever; Belladonna: for flushed face and high temperature; Gelsemium: for a person who feels chilly and may have a dull headache. Consult a qualified homoeopathic practitioner.
• Physiotherapy – tepid baths followed by being wrapped in warm towelling.
• Take herbal teas to expand the energy and also to open the sweat glands to sweat out disease that is located near the surface of the skin.
• Bach flower therapy.

# IMMUNODEFICIENCY/
# AUTO-IMMUNE DISORDERS

Allopathic medicine states that these are a group of conditions in which the immune system fails to function normally, leaving the body open to many infections which would normally be fought by the immune system. Immuno-deficiency disorders are either inherited/congenital, where the immune system fails to develop, or acquired, where damage occurs to the immune system preventing it from functioning normally. Congenital immune disorders affect the adaptive immune system and can lead to persistent thrush (fungus) infections and in severe cases death in babies. Acquired immunodeficiency may result from disease (as in the HIV virus) or suppression of the immune system by drugs. In both cases the body has poor control over invading organisms and tumours. Auto-immune disorders result from the immune system reacting to its own cells and proteins. The cause of this is not fully understood. Rheumatoid arthritis, lupus (systemic lupus erythematosus), rheumatic fever, some forms of anaemia, diabetes mellitus, multiple sclerosis and ulcerative colitis are all examples of auto-immune disorders. Treatment of these conditions is various and based on the presenting symptoms.

According to natural healing methods, immune deficiency arises out of exhaustion. Exhaustion is a result of excessive work, keeping irregular hours coupled with inadequate sleep, and a nutrient deprived diet. When someone is in this state an over-active immune response occurs. Toxins begin to build up, especially in the liver and spleen. The cells can become so degenerated that the body will actually turn on itself as it sees the degenerated cells as a foreign substance that has invaded the body. The person may become oversensitive to normal antigens such as house dust and pollen.

## Glands
Thyroid and adrenals

## Chakras
*Throat* Affirmation – 'I trust and release my need to control my circumstances'
*Solar Plexus* Affirmation – 'I release all negative thoughts and emotions. I am a powerful and open person'

## Emotional cause
The immune system responds to our emotional state. Deep grief can dramatically reduce our immune strength. This emotional energy is associated with the energy of the heart. The brain is also closely aligned with the immune system and certain states of mind can have a powerful effect on the biochemical aspect of the brain. Are you pushing yourself because you need to prove you are worthy? When will you allow yourself to have adequate nourishment and love?

## Reiki treatment

Use position **18** to stimulate the immune system. Also work on positions **6** to **8** for treating the liver, spleen and pancreas, and positions **12** and **13** for adrenal and kidney support.

## Recommended complementary treatment

• Follow a diet that is rich in wholegrains, green vegetables such as spinach, and low-salt white fish.
• Adhere to a balanced lifestyle. Give yourself ample time to work, play, read, meditate, exercise and to enjoy social activity.
• Consult a herbalist for the herbs to support the treatment of immune disorders.
• Supplements – beta-carotene, vitamin B complex, C and E. Minerals: magnesium, selenium and zinc.
• Do yoga for stretching and/or light aerobic exercise such as walking, jogging or cycling four to five times a week.
• Bach flower therapy.

# SWOLLEN GLANDS

According to allopathic medicine, swollen glands are a result of inflammation of the lymph nodes and an abundance of white cells in lymph tissue. They can be caused by infection, allergy and forms of cancer. The most common sites of swollen glands are the neck, armpits and groin. Investigation of the cause is necessary. Further treatment may include medication or, in the case of cancer, surgery and/or radio-therapy.

Natural healing methods state that swollen glands are the body's indicators that it is being overloaded with toxins. When the toxins become excessive the immune system responds. Part of this response also occurs in the adrenal glands. Basically what happens is that the body slows down and your immune system is sluggish, which results in glands that swell and become painful.

## Glands
Thyroid, thymus, adrenals and gonads

## Chakras
*Throat* Affirmation – 'I freely communicate all my thoughts and emotions'
*Sacral Centre* Affirmation – 'I release all conflict that holds me back from my inner harmony'
*Root* Affirmation – 'I accept and acknowledge my right to be here'

## Emotional cause
There is so much going on in life and we often find ourselves confused. Where are the emotional issues that need to be released? What thoughts and feelings are we holding on to that weaken our immune system? When will we say yes to ourselves, even if it means saying no to another person?

## Reiki treatment
Treat the lymph system using positions **19** and **20**, and the immune system stimulation position **18**.

## Recommended complementary treatment
• Eat wholegrains, leafy, green vegetables, root vegetables and fish.
• Do yoga, stretching exercises and go for a gentle walk every day.
• Take warm baths to relax the body so that the lymph glands can drain.
• Bowen body therapy.
• Bach flower therapy.

# TONSILLITIS

According to allopathic medicine, tonsillitis is an infection of the tonsils. Tonsils are made up of lymphatic tissue and are located at the back of the throat. They are an important part of the immune system and protect the upper airways from infection. Treatment includes rest, plenty of fluids, painkillers and occasionally antibiotics. Removal of the tonsils (tonsillectomy), once frequently performed, is now only done in cases of persistent infection or where breathing is obstructed.

From the viewpoint of natural healing methods, the tonsils become inflamed when the blood and lymph vessels become overburdened with toxic waste and bacteria. Once the system is overburdened waste cannot be removed and a swelling of the glands will occur. Other causes are poor diet, poor elimination, and overuse of antibiotics to suppress the common cold which will eliminate friendly flora and weaken the large intestine and immune function.

## Glands
Thyroid, parathyroid, thymus and gonads

## Chakras
**Throat** Affirmation – 'I release my need to control and trust in the process of living'
**Root** Affirmation – 'I am supported and strong'

## Emotional cause
Tonsils are part of the lymphatic and immune systems. They act as filters, monitoring and censoring our reality. If the reality becomes too much to handle and we have intense fear or anger the tonsils will become inflamed. When the tonsils are removed it simply means we have to take in our reality and deal with it in another way inside of ourselves.

## Reiki treatment
Use treatment positions **4** or **4a**, **19** and **20**.

## Recommended complementary treatment
• Eat wholegrains, leafy, green vegetables such as spinach, carrots and carrot juice.
• Avoid eating sweets, highly processed foods, dairy products, wheat and fried foods.
• After you are well again follow a five-day carrot juice fast to clear toxins from the body (see p. 59).
• Consult a qualified homoeopathic practitioner.
• Bach flower therapy.

# 9

# THE
# MUSCULO-
# SKELETAL SYSTEM

**The musculo-skeletal system** of the body comprises two systems, the muscular and the skeletal system. The muscular system refers to a specific type of muscle called skeletal muscle that is primarily attached to bone. It provides movement, stability and heat generation. The skeletal system refers to all the bones, joints and cartilage. It provides structure, support and stability.

There are seven types of skeletal muscle: extensor (opens a joint); flexor (closes a joint); adductor (brings part of the body in); abductor (extends part of body out); levator (raises); depressor (lowers); sphincter (opens and closes around an orifice). The skeletal muscles move by conscious effort in response to chemical messages sent through nerve fibres. Contraction and expansion of muscles around the skeletal system allows the body to move and generates approximately 85 per cent of the body's heat.

The skeletal system functions to provide structure for the body. It protects vital organs; ribs protect the heart and lungs, the skull protects the brain, and the pelvis protects the uterus and bladder. Bones have three layers: an outer thin layer (periosteum) containing blood vessels and nerves; an inner shell (cortical bone) surrounding a spongy layer (cancellous bone). The spaces between cancellous bone

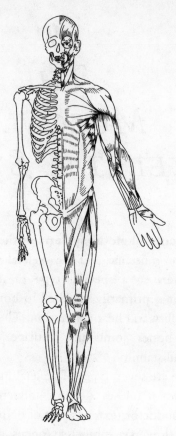

*The musculo-skeletal system*

contain bone marrow, which is responsible for the production of blood cells. Joints are formed when two or more bones meet and allow movement between bones. Types of joints include ball-and-socket (e.g. hip, shoulder), which allow full range of movement; pivot (e.g. neck), which allows rotation only; ellipsoidal (e.g. wrist), which allow all movement except pivotal; and hinge (e.g. knee, elbow), which allow bending and straightening. To reduce friction within joint movement bones are coated with a thin layer of tissue (cartilage) and the joint is encapsulated with tissue, which secretes lubricating fluid. Movable joints also have a fluid-filled sac (bursa) which acts as a pressure cushion. Apart from movable joints there are fixed joints like those between skull bones (sutures).

Disorders of the musculo-skeletal system occur when: (1) there is damage or trauma to muscle tissue, bones and joints; (2) imbalance of the chemical messengers; or (3) infection to the fluids and tissue within the bone, muscle and joints.

Common conditions that can occur in the musculo-skeletal system are arthritis, back pain, leg cramps, bursitis, gout, knee problems, sinusitis, sprains and temporomandibular joint syndrome.

# ARTHRITIS

According to allopathic medicine, arthritis is an inflammation of a joint, characterised by redness, swelling, pain and stiffness. There are seven forms of arthritis:

1) Osteoarthritis results from long-term wear and tear on joints. Primarily this is related to age but there are some hereditary and metabolic factors that cause osteoarthritis.
2) Rheumatoid arthritis is an auto-immune disorder (the body attacks the joint as it would an invading bacterium or virus). It affects the hands, wrists, feet and arms, and occurs mostly in women.
3) Juvenile rheumatoid arthritis (Still's disease) occurs in children under four and usually resolves itself, but may result in permanent deformities.
4) Seronegative arthritis mimics rheumatoid arthritis but is usually associated with auto-immune diseases, and skin and intestinal disorders.
5) Infective arthritis results from the invasion of joints by

bacteria causing an infection of the joint fluids. This may be associated with systemic infections like mumps, rheumatic fever, rubella or chicken pox.

6) Spondylitis is inflammation of the vertebrae and pelvis.
7) Gout occurs when there is a build up of uric acid (a by-product of digestion), which enters a joint and causes inflammation.

Treatment of arthritis depends on the specific variant but includes medication, bed rest, splinting of joints, heat and gentle exercise. In severe cases surgery such as joint replacement (arthroplasty) or fusing the joints (arthrodesis) may be carried out.

Those who follow natural healing methods state that arthritis can be caused by imbalances in the affected tissue. It can also occur because of a high calcium content in the body. The liver may be stagnant due to experiencing too much wind and dampness, resulting in not enough energy being distributed to joints and connective tissue.

## Glands
Thymus (shoulder), gonads (legs)

## Chakras
**Throat and Heart** (shoulder, arms and/or hands)
Affirmation – 'I am open to receive love and communicate my desires'
**Root** (legs) Affirmation – 'I am flexible in my movements and supported in life to move with ease'

## Emotional cause
Arthritis can be seen as a disease that is brought on by rigid thinking, being inflexible, feeling unloved, being critical of oneself or being stubborn. Arthritis can also be brought on by

not being willing to move with the flow of life but having very fixed ideas and opinions about how others and you need to think, act, feel, believe etc. Often you will see people who have been frozen with fear. Their minds are fixed on some sort of fear and they are not able to move away from it. Any thought or emotion that is held on to in such a fixed and rigid manner can eventually manifest as arthritis.

### Reiki treatment
Use positions that can sandwich (one hand above, one below or one hand on one side, one on the other) the joints that are affected. Treat the entire body and then spend extra time on the areas where the arthritis is located. Also use positions **31** to **33** to run energy through the arms and legs.

### Recommended complementary treatment
• Avoid eating dairy products and animal fats.
• Consult a qualified homoeopathic practitioner.
• Hydrotherapy – hot and cold baths will stimulate the circulation.
• Herbal treatments – turmeric (curcumin) is a potent antioxidant and anti-inflammatory.
• Meditate on letting go of structure.
• Bach flower therapy.

# BACK PAIN

According to allopathic medicine, back pain occurs when there is damage to ligaments, muscles and joints or systemic infection. Most people experience some form of back pain at some time, but it is usually resolved before investigations reveal a cause. Chronic back pain usually results from pain and tenderness in the coccyx after a fall (coccygodynia), pressure on the sciatic nerve (sciatica), infection of the kidney (pyelonephritis), degeneration of joints between the spine (osteoarthritis) or pain in the back muscles (fibrositis). Treatment varies, but can include rest, painkillers, anti-inflammatory drugs, muscle relaxants, acupuncture, exercise and physiotherapy.

Natural healing methods state that lower back pain results from many causes but that the most frequent is consistent injury to the kidneys from poor dietary habits and stress. Stress is considered the single most powerful destroyer of energy in the entire system, but especially the muscles of the back. As the kidneys and the related muscles of the low back weaken, the muscles go into spasm. This causes the muscles on either side of the spine to pull unequally on the spinal vertebrae. Eventually the disks and nerves become pinched from the bending movement placed on the spine, and acute pain results. Pain of the middle back is often associated with imbalances in the liver and the spleen. These organs also provide energy for the muscles of the middle back. Upper back pain can be caused by excess kidney energy that is transformed upwards to the neck, or deficient heart energy, or tension in the shoulder muscles caused by stress and liver or gallbladder imbalances. Back pain can also originate from more traditional causes such as lifting heavy objects, prolonged standing, poor posture, lack of exercise, and kidney and reproductive problems.

## Glands
Thyroid, parathyroid, thymus, adrenals and gonads

## Chakras
*Throat* Affirmation – 'I open myself to communicate my desires and trust the process of life'
*Heart* Affirmation – 'I accept unconditional love for myself'
*Solar Plexus* Affirmation – 'I am willing to redefine who I am and what is my reality'

*Sacral Centre* Affirmation – 'I am open and create harmony as a sexual being'

*Root* Affirmation – 'I have the ability to survive, I accept where I am in the world'

## Emotional cause

Back pain is the most complex pain as it is associated with so many emotions and thoughts. What can be happening in your life that is manifesting these problems? Are you faced with tough decisions that will involve finances? Are you feeling unloved? Louise Hay, in *Heal Your Life*, addresses the areas of the back by vertebrae and has a chart of the effects of spinal misalignments. Each vertebra supplies energy to a related area in the body, and if the spine is not aligned properly then pain can manifest as follows:

**Pain in the upper back and neck** can be due to a lack of emotional support, feeling unloved and possibly holding back on giving love to others, and the feeling of being overloaded with responsibility.

**Pain in the middle back** may indicate you are weighed down with guilt, burdened with worry and closed to receiving life's blessings.

**Pain in the lower back** is often associated with a lack of financial support. Also, issues of lack of abundance, sexual matters and feeling trapped under the pressure of keeping up a brave face in times of uncertainty and fear, may be indicated.

## Reiki treatment

Using positions **10** to **14** treat the entire back. Also, if there is low back pain, run energy through the legs using the positions for the sciatic nerve, using positions **24** to **28** to clear the energy in the root chakra down to the feet.

## Recommended complementary treatment

• Avoid excess weight and stress by following a balanced weight reduction programme that includes foods high in wholegrains, fresh vegetables, beans and fruit and low levels of animal fat. This is especially important if the stomach is enlarged as the weight has a tendency to pull on the lower back.

• Review and where possible change the sources of muscle tension: excess sitting; lack of exercise; jobs that require repetitive motion; and stress or repressed emotions, especially anger and fear.

• Take regular aerobic exercise, walking at a brisk pace for at least a half-an-hour each day. Walking is a wonderful way not only to exercise the body, but to reduce stress.

• Use daily stretching exercises to loosen and tone the muscles. Normally this is done when you wake up in the morning.

• Therapeutic massage, hydrotherapy, and hydrotherapy combined with essential oils – hot compresses on the painful part of the back will increase circulation, followed with cold ones to reduce the swelling. Oils in the compresses such as chamomile will have an anti-inflammatory and anti-spasmodic effect, while wintergreen, camphor or eucalyptus help to warm and relax the muscles.

• Acupressure and acupuncture.

• Herbal teas.

• Using meditation and prayer, picture positive outcomes to all situations. See yourself being rather than doing.

• Chiropractic adjustment.

• Bowen body therapy.

• Bach flower therapy.

# BURSITIS

According to modern allopathic medicine, bursitis is an inflammation of the bursa, a fluid-filled cushioning sac surrounding stress points in the body, e.g. joints. The bursa becomes swollen from an excess of fluid, usually resulting from pressure, injury or friction. Occasionally it is linked to infection. Bursitis will generally subside when the affected area is rested. Pain may be managed with ice packs and painkillers. Medication may be prescribed if the cause is attributed to infection. Rarely, surgical intervention is required.

Natural healing methods recognise trauma as being the secondary cause of bursitis. The first cause is stagnation in the joints and liver imbalances. The liver is said to provide energy to the tendons and joins, and is the main aspect to consider when treating bursitis.

## Glands
Adrenals and gonads

## Chakras
**Heart** Affirmation – 'I am open to changes in life. I love and respect myself'
**Solar Plexus** Affirmation – 'In my personal definition I release all emotions and toxins that do not support me'
**Root** Affirmation – 'I move with ease in my life. I am open to change'

## Emotional cause
The liver is the organ where our unexpressed anger and frustration are sited. Bursitis can be inner rage not expressed. We have a need to strike out, yet we are too stiff to do this. Uncertain of what life is bringing us, we hold on to old

thought patterns and are rigid. For healing we need to let go and move with grace.

**Reiki treatment**

Sandwich the joints with both hands. Also run energy using positions **32** and **33**. Use positions **12** and **13** for the kidneys and **7** for the liver.

**Recommended complementary treatment**

• Drink carrot juice to detoxify and support the liver.
• Homoeopathy – Bryony: for pain with motion.
• Hydrotherapy – apply an ice pack to the troubled joint to reduce swelling. Leave it ten minutes several times a day. After the swelling disappears, apply hot towels, as heat will increase the circulation.
• Acupuncture – to open the meridians and increase circulation.
• Acupressure – to stimulate points and massage the tissue.
• Do exercises to loosen the muscles and joints such as arm rotation, reaching up, lifting legs, touching opposite elbows and reaching out.
• Bowen body therapy is particularly effective for joint and muscle pain.

# GOUT

According to allopathic medicine, gout is an arthritic condition of one, or several, joints. It occurs when there is decreased excretion of uric acid in the blood from the urinary system. Excessive uric acid is deposited into joints and crystallises, causing gout. Joints become reddened, inflamed, and swollen, painful and stiff, often restricting movement. Gout occurs as a result of secondary disorders of the kidney, anaemia, side-effects of some medications, and may be inherited. It is treated with rest, occasionally medication and increasing fluid intake.

Natural healing methods view gout as arising from consumption of too much protein-rich food. Protein produces high levels of uric acid, which harms the kidneys and spills over into the blood. Once uric acid is in the blood it accumulates in and around the joints causing an immune reaction and pain. By eliminating high fat and high protein from the diet the symptoms will usually disappear.

## Glands
Adrenals

## Chakras
*Solar Plexus* Affirmation – 'I am safe and secure. I release all negative thought patterns and attitudes'

## Emotional cause
There is not enough love getting in to balance the negative, painful and angry emotions that you continue to hold on to. Gout affects our extremities and joints, which naturally hinders our expression of ourselves out into the world. It also hampers our ability for free and easy movement. What are you being so inflexible about and when will you let it go?

## Reiki treatment
Treat the kidneys and liver using positions **7** and **8**, **12** and **13**. Sandwich all affected joints with both hands.

## Recommended complementary treatment
• Eat green, leafy vegetables such as spinach, kale, cabbage and parsley, bananas, strawberries, celery, vegetable and fruit juices, and purified water.
• Avoid eating excess protein, meat, greasy fried food, yeast and spices.
• T'ai chi is good for circulation and clearing the mind.

- Yoga or stretching exercises.
- Take a walk once a day for twenty to thirty minutes.
- Ride a bicycle every day.
- Supplements – vitamins B complex, C and E.

# KNEE PROBLEMS

Modern allopathic medicine states that disorders of the knee (patella) occur when there is trauma, damage or infection of the joint. Common knee problems are: (1) torn ligaments and cartilage; (2) bleeding into the joint (haemarthrosis); (3) inflamed joint linings (synovitis); (4) inflammation of the fluid-filled sac which cushions the joint (bursitis); (5) arthritis; (6) breaks in the femur or tibia (fractures). Treatment varies but includes rest, painkillers, anti-inflammatory drugs, muscle relaxants, exercise, physiotherapy and, in severe cases, surgery.

According to natural healing methods, knee problems are the result of an imbalance of the deep energy or essence within the kidneys that determines vitality, resistance to disease and longevity. Followers of Chinese medicine call this essence *jing* and also believe a person only has a certain amount, so that when it is used up, we cease to live. The knees can therefore indicate that this vital force energy is low.

## Glands
Adrenals

## Chakras
*Sacral Centre* Affirmation – 'I release my fear and surrender to the movement and direction taking place'

## Emotional cause

The knees are connected to our humility and our flexibility. They are our shock absorbers that allow us to travel over the rough terrain of our lives. What are you afraid of? Perhaps you are being called on to make a big change and are resistant to go with the flow. Make a stand for yourself with humility and grace.

## Reiki treatment

Treat the kidneys with positions **12** and **13**. Also sandwich the knees with both hands and run energy through the entire leg using position **33**.

## Recommended complementary treatment

• Eat fish, cereal, almonds and royal jelly. All of these foods will strengthen the *jing* or essential energy of the kidney.
• Avoid eating fruit, sugar, processed foods, coffee, tea, cocoa, alcohol and excessive amounts of protein.
• Meditation and creative visualisation will release stress, fear, insecurity and overwork. Be in touch with where you are digging in and not surrendering in your life.

# LEG CRAMPS

According to allopathic medicine, a cramp is experienced when a muscle goes into spasm and there is a prolonged period of contraction. Duration of cramps is usually short. They can result from the build-up of chemical by-products from exercise (lactic acid); prolonged repetitive movement or sitting/lying in an awkward position; profuse sweating (due to loss of sodium), e.g. fever or too much heat; and during pregnancy. Treatment includes massage and stretching, and in some cases medication may be prescribed.

Those who follow natural healing methods view leg cramps as indicating typically weak and tired kidneys, along with a depletion of essential minerals and antioxidants, especially magnesium and vitamin E.

## Glands
Adrenals and gonads

## Chakras
*Solar Plexus* Affirmation – 'I am flexible. I respond to my inner urge to change'
*Root* Affirmation – 'I take a stand for myself and am supported in my process of change'

## Emotional cause
Our legs are what move us forward in the world. We take the creative impulse of the sacral centre and actualise it with our legs. Perhaps we are going in a direction that no longer supports us or we feel like we have hit a wall and can no longer go forward. We are mentally confused as to what is right for us and perhaps feel that we are not on solid ground. Take a moment to come back into your centre and move with the flow of life.

## Reiki treatment
Use positions **12** and **13** to treat the kidneys; positions **22** and **24** to treat the root chakra; and **33** to run energy through the legs.

## Recommended complementary treatment
• Eat beans, white fish, green and leafy vegetables, fresh fruit juice, fresh vegetable juice and grains.
• Avoid eating meat, soft drinks and dairy products.
• Use meditation and creative visualisation to find where the fear is or what change you are resisting and see the way opening up for you.

- Bowen body therapy.
- Bach flower therapy.

# SINUSITIS

Allopathic medicine states that sinusitis is an infection of the facial sinuses secondary to the common cold or less frequently an abscess (collection of pus) in an upper tooth. The sinuses are pockets of air space surrounding the nose. There are seven sinuses in the face: one either side of the nose (maxillary); one either side of the tip of the nose (ethmoidal); one between the eyes (sphenoidal); and one each side above the eyes (frontal). Most commonly affected are the maxillary and ethmoidal. Sinusitis is a common condition and may be treated with antibiotics, decongestant drugs and, in severe cases, surgery to drain the sinus.

According to natural healing methods, a sinus condition can indicate a problem with the large intestine being blocked up with accumulated waste. When the problem becomes chronic then sinusitis can develop. Also, if the diet is mostly acidic, this will cause the spleen to become imbalanced.

## Glands
Pituitary, thalamus and adrenals

## Chakras
*Third Eye* Affirmation – 'I release any negative ways of seeing my life's process'
*Solar Plexus* Affirmation – 'I release all negative thoughts and emotions that are toxic to me'
*Root* Affirmation – 'I am fully supported by life'

### Emotional cause
Sinusitis can indicate a deep emotional and mental conflict that results in our inability to communicate. Usually this involves someone to whom we are close. What is this dripping emotion that you are holding on to?

### Reiki treatment
Use treatment positions **1**, **8**, **18**, **19** and **20**.

### Recommended complementary treatment
• Eat foods such as wholegrains, vegetables, fruit and carrot juices.
• Follow a five-day dairy-product-free diet which will help cleanse mucus.
• Use Chinese medicine to boost the immune system, strengthen the large intestine, spleen and lungs, and also improve bowel function.
• Acupressure.
• Acupuncture.
• Shiatsu massage.
• Bach flower therapy.

## SPRAINS

According to modern allopathic medicine, a sprain is a tear or stretching of the tissues (ligaments) that hold bone ends together in joints. The capsule that encases the joint may also be affected. It is usually caused by traumatic stress to the affected joint. The most common site of injury is the ankle. Sprains produce pain and swelling around the joint and may also involve some degree of muscle spasm. Initial treatment requires the application of a cold pack and compression (tight bandage). The affected limb should be elevated and kept still. Gentle exercise should only begin when the sprain is no longer painful. Serious cases may require surgical repair and/or treatment with anti-inflammatory medication.

According to natural healing methods, sprains occur from a traumatic incident. The underlying cause is an area of imbalance due to too much or too little life force energy in that area. A sprain requires that you stop to rest and come back into the centre of who you are.

## Glands
Depends on the area of trauma

## Chakras
Depends on the area of trauma

## Emotional cause
Usually when we sprain a muscle in the wrist or ankle, it indicates a mental sprain as well. We have gone as far as we can with this particular mind set and a sprain results. Are you moving in a direction that truly supports you or is it the time to change direction? Are you standing on unstable ground and need to build a new foundation for your life?

## Reiki treatment
Sandwich the affected area with both of your hands.

## Recommended complementary treatment
• Rub Arnica tincture on the sprain.
• Homoeopathy – Bryonia: for swelling; Arnica: for initial shock.
• Apply ice to the area to reduce the swelling and elevate the part that is sprained. Once the swelling has gone down place the injured spot in hot water or apply moist hot compresses to promote circulation.

- Take Bach flower Rescue Remedy internally – four drops straight from the bottle using the dispenser tip.
- Apply Bach flower Rescue Cream to the sprain.

# TEMPOROMANDIBULAR-JOINT (TMJ) SYNDROME

According to modern allopathic medicine, temporomandibular joint (TMJ) syndrome is a collection of symptoms that affect the joint between the head (temperal bone) and the jaw (mandible). It occurs when the TMJ and the surrounding muscles and ligaments do not function normally. It is thought to be caused by spasm of the muscles involved in chewing, or clenching and grinding teeth when emotionally stressed. Dislocation of the jaw as a result of trauma of the head or neck may be a causal factor. The syndrome is marked by headaches, tender jaw muscles and dull, aching facial pain, which increases in strength around the ear. Treatment includes application of a heat pack, muscle relaxants, massage, eating soft foods, wearing a device at night to prevent grinding of the jaw, counselling, biofeedback, and relaxation training. Surgery may be required in severe cases.

Problems related to the jaw are seen by those who follow natural healing methods as imbalances in the kidney, bladder, sex organs and stomach meridians. The body with its wisdom sees the jaw as the place to discharge excessive energy because it is so active. Oriental medicine connects grinding the teeth and jaw with an expression of frustration, often sexual frustration.

**Glands**
Pituitary, thyroid, thalamus and adrenals

## Chakras
*Third Eye* Affirmation – 'I see creative ways to express my anger and frustation'
*Throat* Affirmation – 'I am open and expressive'
*Solar Plexus* Affirmation – 'I release all frustration and tension'

## Emotional cause
The teeth and jaw are closely connected. When we tighten our jaw we are also clenching our teeth. This way we stop swallowing and are able to hold on to everything just as it is without changing. We grind our teeth in anger and we pull back our jaw for the same reason. When will you let go of frustration and anger and relax your jaw?

## Reiki treatment
Lay your hands on the jaw using position **16**. Treat the liver, kidneys, sex organs and bladder using positions **6** to **9**, **12** and **13**.

## Recommended complementary treatment
- Use meditation to relax.
- Therapeutic massage.
- Acupressure along the spine, low back, head and neck.
- Acupuncture.
- Yoga.

# 10

# THE REPRODUCTIVE SYSTEM – FEMALE AND MALE

**The female and male reproductive** system comprises organs, tissues and cells that work in complement to produce offspring. The female reproductive system consists of ovaries, uterine (fallopian) tubes, uterus, vagina, vulva and mammary glands. The male reproductive system consists of the testes, scrotum, epididymis, vas deferens, seminal vesicle, urethra, prostate gland and penis.

## HUMAN REPRODUCTION CYCLE

**Both the male and female** produce gametes (sex cells). In the female the gamete is called an ovum; in the male it is the sperm. When an ovum is fertilised by a sperm the union results in a new cell called a zygote (fertilised ovum). A zygote attaches to the uterus and develops into an embryo (early human life). In later development this is called a foetus. Once the foetus is born it is referred to as a newborn or baby.

The ovaries are the sites of ova (multiple of ovum) development. They are located on each side of the uterus. Approximately once a month an ovum is released into the fallopian tubes. At the same time hormones produced by the ovaries alter the lining of the uterus for possible implantation

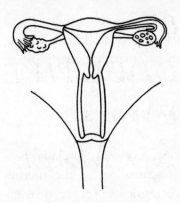

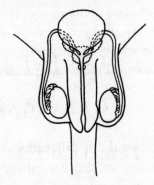

*Female reproductive organs*          *Male reproductive organs*

by a zygote. If, during its travel from the fallopian tube into the uterus, the ovum meets and is joined with a sperm, then the newly formed zygote attaches to the uterine wall and begins developing into an embryo and then on to a foetus. If the ovum is not fertilised by sperm the levels of hormone decrease and the lining of the uterus is expelled (menstruation). If a zygote is implanted then secretions from the placenta maintain the levels of hormones. Nutrients are passed on from the mother to the foetus via the umbilical cord. Once the foetus is born the placenta and other products of pregnancy are expelled (referred to as the afterbirth) and the uterus returns to its previous structure and function.

The site of gamete (sperm) production in the male is the testis. Sperm cells are in continual production and released from the testes during male orgasm. As the sperm leaves the testes it is mixed with secretions from the testes, seminal vesicles, prostate gland, and bulbourethral gland and is called semen. The rhythmic contractions of orgasm force semen out of the penis through the urethra. Millions of sperm cells enter the uterus through the erect penis, which is placed inside the vagina during sexual intercourse. Sperm cells survive up to forty-eight hours inside the uterine environment.

Common conditions of the reproductive system dealt with in this section are cervical dysplasia, fibrocystic breast disease, fibrocystic uterus (fibroid tumours) infertility, menopause, menstrual problems, prostate problems and yeast infections.

# CERVICAL DYSPLASIA

According to allopathic medicine, cervical dysplasia is a change in the size, shape and organisation of the uterine cervical wall cells. This is often a result of prolonged irritation or inflammation of the cervix. The condition usually reverses when the cause of irritation or inflammation is removed. If left untreated it may advance and develop into a benign or malignant tumour. Cervical dysplasia has been linked to viral infections on the penis of male sex partners. Early detection of cellular changes can be achieved through regular cervical smears which examine microscopically cells taken from the cervix. Abnormal cells are destroyed either by electrocoagulation (heat) or cryosurgery (cold). Severe cases will require medical and/or surgical intervention. Cervical smears should be a regular component of a woman's health maintenance programme.

According to natural healing methods, an abnormal cervical smear may indicate stagnation and inadequate energy in the kidneys, bladder and sex organs. The underlying factors that support the growth of abnormal cells may be psychological. These factors may indicate some form of trauma, such as one or more abortions, a history of sexual trauma or an excessive number of sexual partners. Abnormal cells indicate a pre-cancerous condition or early stages of cancer, but can usually be reversed with natural therapy.

**Glands**
Adrenals and ovaries

## Chakras
*Sacral* Affirmation – 'I release all past trauma and judgements and fully open my sexual side'
*Root* Affirmation – 'I am supported emotionally, mentally and physically in my life's journey'

## Emotional cause
A pre-cancerous condition such as this suggests an accumulation through the years of inner conflict, guilt, hurt, grief, resentment and confusion in association with sexuality. Past sexual trauma held on to creates a rejection of that part of us. Do you feel able to deal with the deep-seated issues that are represented here?

## Reiki treatment
Use positions **9** and **29** to treat reproductive disorders. Treat two or three times a week for a month and then decrease to once a week. Suggest that the client take a Reiki class so she can also treat herself.

## Recommended complementary treatment
• Take aerobic exercise such as walking, cycling, swimming or jogging three to five times a week to promote more energy in the body and a clearer mind.
• Meditate on the tension held in the pelvic area to discover the root of the tension. Ask your body 'What are you trying to tell me?' Satisfy the needs of your inner being that may be holding on to fear and pain.
• Use creative visualisation with imaging exercises that promote faith and openness.
• Hydrotherapy – alternate hot and cold sitz baths to promote local circulation. Do this two to three times a day.
• Bach flower therapy.

# FIBROCYSTIC
# BREAST DISEASE

According to allopathic medicine, fibrocystic breast disease is the primary cause of breast lumps in women. Cysts, fluid-filled sacs, develop in breast tissue and milk-secreting cells, causing lumps to appear. They are often more noticeable before menstruation when breasts become lumpy, tender and swollen. The condition has been linked to levels of hormones involved in the reproductive cycle. Early detection of lumps can be achieved through regular self-examination. Only rarely do cysts develop into cancer of the breast but all breast lumps should be investigated. It should be noted that males also have breast tissue, however the incidence of breast cancer in males is significantly lower than in females. A doctor may aspirate cysts to relieve pain. Medication may also be prescribed.

According to natural healing methods, high fat in the Western diet is the cause of fibrocystic breast disease. This high fat diet increases the female hormone oestrogen. Fat cells produce oestrogen. A diet that is high in fats and low in fibre causes a build-up of toxicity in the body. When oestrogen levels are lowered in the body the lumps usually disappear.

**Glands**
Thymus

**Chakras**
*Heart* Affirmation – 'I am open to life's pleasures and fully love and forgive myself'

**Emotional cause**
Fibrocystic breast disease is deeply connected to love and to a

sense of self-identity. It tends to indicate deep mental thought patterns and attitudes that have often been there since childhood. These centre on being a woman and the freedom to express yourself as a woman. The breasts are the most outward expression of femininity. It is from the breasts that a woman is able to nourish others as well as to appear soft and intimate. Any conflict of emotions surrounding her idea of nourishing or self-worth can show up here.

## Reiki treatment
Use positions **20** and **21** to treat the breasts and the lymph system. Start treatment about two weeks before the menstrual cycle and finish when the period begins. Suggest that women with this problem take a Reiki course to enable them to work with it.

## Recommended complementary treatment
• Stop taking birth control pills as they contain oestrogen – the cause of cysts in the breasts. Use alternative birth control methods. Have your oestrogen levels checked and take steps to reduce high levels.
• Eat wholegrains, fresh vegetables, tofu, tempeh and carrot juice. Increase your fibre intake as this combines with oestrogen in the intestine and eliminates it from the body. Eat foods that detoxify the liver such as dandelion greens and dandelion tea.
• Avoid eating red meat, dairy products, eggs, fried foods, coffee, tea, cola and chocolate to reduce cholesterol levels.
• Write down in a journal your feelings about being a woman. List positive thoughts about yourself and the qualities you acknowledge in yourself for each day. This is positive reinforcement.
• Use meditation to relax. Visualise yourself as a warm, sensual, creative woman who loves herself.

• Chinese medicine will open and release stagnation of the liver meridian.

# FIBROCYSTIC UTERUS

According to allopathic medicine, fibroids are abnormal growths of tissue in the uterus. Their size can vary; thus the effect on uterine function can differ. Most small fibroids go unnoticed. Larger ones, however, are often unveiled when investigating abnormal menstruation, pain and discomfort of the bladder and bowel, frequent miscarriages or infertility. The cause of fibroids is unknown, however enlargement of fibroids may result from changes in hormone levels as a result of oral contraceptives containing oestrogen (female hormone) or pregnancy. Small fibroids are monitored for changes. Large fibroids adversely affecting body function require surgical intervention.

Natural healing methods view fibroids as stagnated blood due to insufficient circulation in the reproductive area. The stagnant blood congeals and forms tumours. Therefore natural healing remedies are designed to increase the energy in the reproductive area and promote healthy circulation. It is thought that a diet high in oestrogen-producing fat and low in fibre is the leading cause of fibroids. When a woman enters menopause the fibroids normally shrink in size.

## Glands
Ovaries

## Chakras
*Sacral* Affirmation – 'I release all unexpressed hurt, guilt, shame and anger from my past. I love being a woman'
*Root* Affirmation – 'I am fully supported and rejoice in being a feminine woman'

## Emotional cause

A lump of soft tissue represents a mass of mental attitudes or patterns that have been suppressed over a long period of time, such that they now have taken solid form. The womb is connected to our feelings of being a woman, especially about our femininity, sexuality and of becoming a mother. All accumulated and unexpressed guilt, shame, inner confusion and abuse are held in the womb and can become fibroids. If we have enough fear about becoming a mother or have unexpressed emotions about ourselves as women, fibroids can stop pregnancy from taking place.

## Reiki treatment

Use positions **9** and **29** to work directly over the area of the womb. Treat during the most fertile period, i.e. approximately two weeks before the onset of the period. Recommend that the woman takes a Reiki course so that she can work with herself.

## Recommended complementary treatment

• The following spices and foods can have a dispersing effect on stagnated blood: ginger, cayenne, nutmeg, white pepper, rosemary and basil; chives, garlic, spring onions, leeks, aubergines, adzuki beans, seaweed and kohlrabi.
• Avoid eating meat, dairy products, eggs, sweets, cold food and drinks.
• Meditation with creative visualisation – place your hands over your womb and visualise all negative and unexpressed emotions leaving this area and replace them with affirming thoughts of being a woman.
• T'ai chi.
• Journal writing – take the time to write out areas of shame, guilt and anger to make room for new thoughts.
• Join women's support groups moderated by a trained

therapist if there has been a problem with abuse and guilt.
• Bach flower therapy.

# INFERTILITY

According to modern allopathic medicine, infertility refers to
the inability of two people to conceive a child. Infertility
results from an alteration in the normal functioning of the
male or female reproductive system. Both partners need to be
assessed for fertility. Male infertility is primarily due to absent
or low sperm production, or abnormal sperm growth and
development. Causes of male infertility include damage or
blockage of the reproductive organs, endocrine disorders,
effects of sexually transmitted diseases, inflammation of the
testes, decreased sperm count secondary to smoking and
some drugs, or genetic disorders such as cystic fibrosis.
Treating male infertility is not frequently successful, but low
sperm counts may be assisted in some cases with medication.
Female infertility can result from an absence or blockage of
the fallopian tubes, failure of the ovaries to produce or release
ova, abnormalities of the uterus which prevent implantation
of the zygote, or mucus produced by the cervix may destroy
a partner's sperm. Treatment of female infertility has a more
favourable outcome. Hormones may be used to stimulate ova
to be released into the fallopian tubes. Surgery may restore
function to damaged fallopian tubes. In vitro fertilisation
mixes ova with sperm outside of the body which are returned
to the uterus for possible implantation, in cases of dysfunc-
tional or absent fallopian tubes, low male sperm counts or
when cervical mucus destroys sperm cells. Other methods of
artificial conception may also be used.

Before undertaking any natural healing methods it is
imperative that the couple has a complete physical examination by a medical fertility specialist to rule out any

complications and to ensure both parties are healthy. The belief is that infertility is due to a yang energy deficiency in the kidneys and this can be treated by a person trained in Chinese medicine.

## Glands
Adrenals and gonads

## Chakras
*Solar Plexus* Affirmation – 'I am strong in my desire to create and sustain a new life'
*Sacral* Affirmation – 'I am a sensual and open person'
*Root* Affirmation – 'I am stable and supported by life'

## Emotional cause
Many couples experiencing difficulties in conceiving are mostly living in their past or future. There is very little time spent in the here and now which is the creative moment. They have forgotten how to enjoy each other and the time they are together. The act of lovemaking is just for procreation. Doubt arises about their ability and completeness. Let yourselves go and trust in the creative process. Play and be with each other without demanding that anything be the result of this time you are together. Often when couples relax and give up trying to have a baby they conceive. The demand is what gets in the way.

## Reiki treatment
Using positions **9** and **29**, treat the reproductive areas of both the man and woman. Also treat the kidneys using positions **12** and **13**.

## Recommended complementary treatment
• Both partners should follow a neutral diet (neither too salty

nor too sweet) to help them to come into harmony with their energy. This will stabilise the semen and moisture from the vagina.

- Massage.
- Aromatherapy.
- Take exercise such as swimming, walking and jogging.
- Vitamin supplements.
- Exercises in communication and touch, and experiences in sensuality, are helpful.
- Bach flower therapy.

# MENOPAUSE

According to allopathic medicine, menopause refers to the cessation of menstruation in women. Usually occuring at around forty-five to fifty years it is marked by halted ova production, and changes in oestrogen and other hormone levels. Psychophysical symptoms result from these changes. Psychologically, women may experience poor concentration, tearfulness, decreased interest in sex and/or depression. Physically, menopausal women experience 'hot flushes', vaginal dryness and/or a frequent need to urinate. Osteoporosis (decreased bone density and increased brittle-ness) and increased fat levels in blood can also result from the effect of menopausal changes. The psychophysical effects of menopause have been successfully treated with hormone replacement therapies.

For those who follow natural healing methods, menopause marks the cessation of menstruation and an important step in the maturation of women. In most cultures it is considered a rite of passage brought on by the reduction of oestrogen production. It can be celebrated as a new and freer way of living, depending on one's personal outlook on life.

## Glands
Ovaries

## Chakras
*Solar Plexus* Affirmation – 'I am no longer dependent on others' impressions about me. I live in harmony with myself'
*Sacral Centre* Affirmation – 'I am sensual and respond to my creative side easily'
*Root* Affirmation – 'I embrace the changes in me and am free to make new steps in my life'

## Emotional cause
Menopause can be quite emotionally charged as the body makes changes. The reaction to hot flushes, night sweats and emotional highs and lows will depend on how much space you are giving yourself to feel this newness. If you are in denial about your ageing process it may be a harder time for you. The single most important thing is to honour yourself and to see the possibilities of a freer lifestyle coupled with finding the woman inside who has gone past the procreative abilities and has found a deeper purpose for living. Your rebirth is here.

## Reiki treatment
Treat using positions **9** and **29** for reproductive support, and use positions **12** and **13** to stimulate the adrenals.

## Recommended complementary treatment
• A diet low in fat and high in fibre will help the body adjust more easily to changing hormonal levels.
• Eat royal jelly to tone the female hormonal system, beans, tofu, carrots, apples and yams.
• Avoid animal proteins and fat, sugar and refined foods. Coffee and alcohol can cause hot flushes.

• Homoeopathy – Pulsatilla: for frequent mood changes; Sepia: for emotional exhaustion. Consult a qualified homoeopathic practitioner.
• Take aerobic exercise such as walking, dance, t'ai chi and tennis.
• Walk on wet grass or lean your back against a tree, as both are grounding exercises that you can do to support yourself emotionally.
• Bach flower therapy.

# MENSTRUAL PROBLEMS

According to allopathic medicine, a delicate balance of uterine wall lining development and hormone regulation controls menstruation. Changes in normal menstruation can be indicative of underlying problems. Dysmenorrhoea (painful periods) is common, but the cause is unknown, while amenorrhoea (the absence of periods) occurs during pregnancy, and through stress, starvation and anorexia. Excessive bleeding (menorrhagia) may be a result of hormone imbalance, inter-uterine contraceptives, fibroids or polyps (tissue growth). Menstruation problems should be investigated medically and are treated according to cause, including by medication, diet modification and, in some cases, surgery.

Natural healing methods state that a medical doctor must first check out irregularities in the menstrual cycle. After any serious illness has been ruled out, the underlying causes can be addressed. Women with premenstrual syndrome, breast tenderness and imbalanced periods (especially those with heavy bleeding) usually have high oestrogen levels. Typically diets are found to be rich in fat and cholesterol. There has also been an increase in young women starting their first periods before the age of twelve because of high oestrogen levels in their blood. Taking birth control pills that disrupt the natural cycle also affect the adrenal glands which produce 20 per cent of a woman's oestrogen.

## Glands
Adrenals and ovaries

## Chakras
*Solar Plexus* Affirmation – 'I am safe as a woman in this world'
*Sacral Centre* Affirmation – 'I am feminine, sensual and open to life'

## Emotional cause
A monthly period is a reminder to women that they are females living in a largely male-dominated world. They are busy in careers that require at times for them to put away their femininity and be stronger. Yet it is expected that they will pick up the woman's role when they return home at night. It can be confusing to be at opposite extremes. Also, if there has been any history of sexual abuse this can cause problems with menstruation, as there is a denial of the feminine aspect out of the need to be safe. What are your deepest feelings about being a woman?

## Reiki treatment
Use positions **9** and **29** for reproductive disorders, **7** and **8** for bowel support, and **22** for the low back pain that often accompanies menstruation.

## Recommended complementary treatment
• Avoid eating red meat, highly salted foods, sugar, dairy fat and caffeine.
• Homoeopathy – Belladonna, Pulsatilla or Sepia. Consult a qualified homoeopathic practitioner.

• Take supplements such as beta-carotene, vitamins B complex, C and E, and calcium, magnesium and zinc.
• Essential oils.
• Avoid heavy emotional stress.
• Enjoy outdoor exercises such as swimming.
• Do abdominal exercises to strengthen the uterus.
• Bach flower therapy.

## PROSTATE PROBLEMS

According to allopathic medicine, the prostate gland is located around the opening of the urethra in males, and its main functions are to provide lubrication for the urethra and to secrete fluid to mix with semen during ejaculation. Prostatitis is an inflammation of the prostate from bacterial infection, sometimes as a result of sexually transmitted diseases. Normally antibiotics are prescribed for this. Enlarged prostate can occur in older males, causing obstruction of the urethra and difficulties in urination. Surgical intervention may be required to decrease the size of the prostate. Cancer of the prostate can occur in young males; however, it is more prevalent in the elderly. It usually exhibits similar symptoms to an enlarged prostate. Depending on the severity of the cancer, surgery and radiotherapy may be required. Medication may also be used to control the growth of the prostate.

Natural healing methods state that stress and lifestyle, together with a diet that is high in animal protein and saturated fats, are important factors in prostate problems. According to Chinese medicine, prostate problems are considered to stem from a weakened kidney meridian as the kidneys provide energy to the prostate.

## Glands
Adrenals and gonads

## Chakras
*Sacral Centre* Affirmation – 'I am a sensual man who is capable of living and sharing myself with others'
*Root* Affirmation – 'I am fully supported in my life. All that I need is provided for me'

## Emotional cause
The prostate is related to our sense of power and capability. Problems often occur in older men who may start to feel less at ease and dissatisfied with their sexual performance. Many men at this age feel frustrated, impotent, confused and start searching for younger partners or just give up altogether. Our sexual expression reflects our inner feelings.

## Reiki treatment
Treat using the prostate treatment position **22**.

## Recommended complementary treatment
• Take exercise such as walking and active aerobic sports that require the body to twist and turn.
• Do a daily yoga routine and stretching exercises that focus on stretching the pelvic region.
• Meditate, pray, or relax daily to relieve stress. Participate in any religious organisation that will strengthen your faith if that is important to you.
• Supplements – vitamins E and C.
• Consult a qualified homoeopathic practitioner.
• Bach flower therapy.

# YEAST INFECTIONS (CANDIDIASIS)

According to allopathic medicine, the fungus candida albicans is the usual cause of yeast infections. It is most common in women around the vagina; however, rarely it occurs around the penis head of uncircumcised males. It is characterised by a white discharge, accompanied by itching, and may involve difficulties in urination. Generally the infection is treated with anti-fungal medications. It is also important to keep areas clean and dry. Treatment of sexual partners is also recommended to prevent cross-infection.

Natural healing methods maintain that yeast infections are now a rampant problem around the world. Most women at one time or another suffer with yeast infections or candidiasis. When the body is healthy the immune system and the bacterial environment keep candida in check, preventing it from growing into a disease state. However, antibiotics, diet and stress levels have weakened the immune system so that yeast infections can flourish.

## Glands
Thymus, adrenals and ovaries

## Chakras
*Heart* Affirmation – 'I open to receive all life's abundant blessings'
*Solar Plexus* Affirmation – 'I know I am safe and nourished in physical relationships'
*Sacral Centre* Affirmation – 'I have opened to intimacy and sexual expression'
*Root* Affirmation – 'I am supported to move forward in my life'

## Emotional cause

In this situation what weakens the body's immunity and causes a yeast infection is our unexpressed conflicts concerning our sexuality, our sexual activity or our ability to be intimate and share this part of ourselves. If this situation arises during an intense relationship, it may be because outer issues are coming up as a result of being intimate and open with another person. Perhaps we have been sexually abused or are feeling abused now. This is an irritation of our sexual nature. Having candida also gives us the time and space to evaluate why this is happening.

## Reiki treatment

Use positions **6** to **8** to treat the liver and intestines. Use positions **9** and **29** to treat the reproductive area. Use positions **19** and **20** to treat the lymphatic system, and position **18** to stimulate the immune system.

## Recommended complementary treatment

• Avoid the following foods because they promote the growth of yeast: sugar, mushrooms, eggs, yeast and products containing yeast, cheese, dairy products and meat.
• Drink aloe vera juice four times a day.
• Use meditation to relax.
• Use creative visualisation techniques for clearing any past fear and making a new future.
• Do t'ai chi for relaxation and movement.

# *11*
# THE RESPIRATORY SYSTEM

**The respiratory system** of the body comprises an upper respiratory tract (nose, mouth, throat, larynx and sinus cavities) and a lower respiratory tract (windpipe, bronchi, diaphragm and lungs). Its prime function is, in conjunction with the cardiovascular system, to exchange gases (oxygen and carbon dioxide) between the blood and the lungs. Its secondary function is to filter air, produce sounds and aid in water elimination. The receptors for the sense of smell are also located in the upper respiratory tract.

The exchange of gases between the lungs and blood is known as respiration. Respiration begins with inspiration (inflow of air). Air from the atmosphere is taken into the mouth and nose and passed down the pharynx (throat) and larynx (voice box) and into the trachea (windpipe). There it travels down the left and right bronchi into the lungs (consisting of bronchioles and alveolar sacs). Oxygen is taken from the atmospheric air and passed into the bloodstream. Concurrently carbon dioxide is released from the blood and taken into the lungs. During expiration the waste products of respiration are expelled out of the lungs, into the bronchi, back up the trachea, past the larynx and pharynx, and out of the nose and mouth.

Common conditions of the respiratory system dealt with in this section are asthma, bronchitis, common cold, cough, hiccups, influenza and sore throat.

---

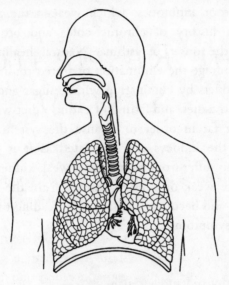

*The respiratory system*

# ASTHMA

According to allopathic medicine, asthma is a recurrent inflammation of the bronchi and bronchioles causing constriction. The inflammation also increases production of phlegm (sputum) which further narrows air passages. Symptoms of asthma include breathlessness, wheezing and cough. Asthma often develops in childhood but resolves later in life. Exercise, infection, pollen, dust and stress that would not otherwise affect another person can bring asthma attacks on. Management includes preventive and treatment medication, and avoidance of contact with triggers.

Those who follows natural healing methods see people with asthma as those who may have been weaned too early, usually before they are one year old. They may also suffer from hypoglycaemia and/or have excessive amounts of dairy, sugar and wheat products in their diets. Research also indicates that problems with asthma may arise if a child has taken high doses of antibiotics, which weaken the auto-immune system. A history of chronic colds and bronchitis often proceeds the onset of asthma. Natural healing modalities often encourage the elimination of stored toxins, mucus and waste products by eliminating wheat, sugar and dairy products from the diet, and fasting or eating a diet with no animal protein or fat in order to cleanse the system. In Chinese medicine the kidneys are stimulated as it is thought that people who suffer from asthma have weak kidneys. When the kidneys are weak or stressed, energy from the lungs cannot pass freely and becomes stagnant, thus leading to the onset of asthmatic symptoms.

## Glands
Pituitary, thyroid and adrenals

## Chakras
*Third Eye* Affirmation – 'I open my intuition and use my ability to see clearly'
*Throat* Affirmation – 'I trust the process of life'
*Heart* Affirmation – 'I have unconditional love for myself'
*Solar Plexus* Affirmation – 'I am defining who I am and what is my reality'

## Emotional cause
Asthma seems to occur most often when a child feels there is not enough room emotionally to breathe. Their need for space is often not seen because of over-mothering. The child may be experiencing a smothering type of love which can lead to the child having a feeling of being choked. These children appear weak and are usually timid, often being manipulated as in 'mother knows best'. By the time they are in early adulthood, they may find themselves standing on their own feet, and having established their boundaries and

what they need, so that the symptoms begin to disappear.

### Reiki treatment

Treat these positions to harmonise the following: upper chest, position **4**; the immune system, position **18**; lung and respiratory problems, position **21**; the kidneys, positions **12** and **13**.

### Recommended complementary treatment

• Avoid eating dairy products, sugar and wheat; eliminate coffee, tea and alcohol from your diet.
• Define and create your boundaries with meditation.
• Use t'ai chi to help expend personal energy.
• Bach flower therapy.

# BRONCHITIS

According to allopathic medicine, bronchitis is an infection of the bronchi identified by frequent coughing which produces phlegm (sputum). It is caused by airborne organisms entering the bronchi. However, the leading causes of chronic bronchitis are smoking and pollution. Treatment includes plenty of fluids, steam inhalation and, in some cases, medication.

Those who follow natural healing methods view bronchitis as resulting from repeated suppression of the common cold through the use of antibiotics and other forms of medication. Natural healing methods maintain that the main causes of bronchitis are poor diet, especially excess sugar, lack of exercise and the accumulation of toxins in the lungs and bronchial passages that irritate the tissues and cause inflammation.

## Glands
Thyroid, parathyroid, thymus and adrenals

## Chakras
*Throat* Affirmation – 'I open and release my emotions and communicate my needs'
*Heart* Affirmation – 'I am open to receiving and giving love and joy'
*Solar Plexus* Affirmation – 'I can release thoughts and emotions that are toxic to my body and myself'

## Emotional cause
It is thought that bronchitis stems from an inflamed family atmosphere. Family can be immediate, but you also have a work family and a family of friends. In all cases, if the atmosphere is inflamed with arguments and yelling sometimes bronchitis will be the result. It could also be the result of an emotionally charged yet silent atmosphere. The power of the unspoken word can cause disharmony. For healing to occur there is a need for personal space and definition of what will allow you to breathe and express yourself fully.

## Reiki treatment
Use positions **4**, **5** and **6** to support the upper chest and respiratory area.

## Recommended complementary treatment
• Avoid eating dairy products as these will increase the phlegm in the lung area.
• Use Chinese medicine specifically with regard to lung conditions.
• Drink Yerba Santa as a tea to stimulate all digestive juices. This is good for all types of bronchitis.
• Homoeopathy – Ipecac: for violent and spasmodic cough;

Belladonna: for a short, dry cough; Pulsatilla: for the gagging cough that is dry in the evening and loose in the morning. Consult a qualified homoeopathic practitioner.
• Hydrotherapy – use a combination of pine, olbas oil and eucalyptus oil added to boiling water. Make a tent covering you and the bowl. Inhale the vapours of steam.
• Bach flower therapy.

# COMMON COLDS

Modern allopathic medicine defines a common cold as an infection of the lining of the mouth, nose and throat. Symptoms include sneezing, runny nose, nasal congestion, cough, sore throat and headache. Colds are caused by a group of viruses called rhinovirus and coronavirus. Treatment is symptomatic and includes rest, plenty of fluids, paracetamol, nasal decongestants, steam inhalation and throat lozenges. Only in severe cases are antibiotics prescribed.

In natural healing methods a cold is considered a natural way for the body to cleanse and detoxify itself. The cold rids the body of accumulated waste. Waste products weaken the immune system and create the foothold needed for the virus to work in the body. Often in allopathic medicine, medication is given to reduce symptoms or to stop the cleansing process. This actually works against the system as it drives the waste products further into the system. More rest and fluids need to be taken to support the body's process of internal cleansing.

**Glands**
Thalamus, thyroid, parathyroid, thymus and adrenals

**Chakras**
*Third Eye* Affirmation – 'I open my intuitive process to find what thoughts have blocked me'

*Throat* Affirmation – 'I express all my emotions and release my need to control myself'

*Heart* Affirmation – 'I am open to receiving and giving love. I release any pain that is stored there'

*Solar Plexus* Affirmation – 'I release all toxins, including toxic thoughts and emotions'

*Sacral Centre* Affirmation – 'I am in perfect harmony with all aspects of myself'

### Emotional cause

Have you been doing too much? Have you stressed your body beyond its maximum capabilities? Catching a cold can also indicate that you need time to integrate your life experiences. Where are the emotional issues that need to be released? What thoughts and feelings are you holding on to that weaken your immune system? When will you say yes to yourself even if it means saying no to another person?

### Reiki treatment

Use position **1** to help clear any sinus blockage, position **4** for the throat, position **5** for the upper chest, and positions **6** to **8** for the spleen, liver and colon. Also use position **18** to strengthen the immune system.

### Recommended complementary treatment

• Get plenty of rest, drink plenty of fluids. Keep lighting low and keep warm.

• Respect the demands of your body. This is not a time to push yourself. Use this time to establish a healthy way to support your body, mind and spirit.

• Homoeopathy – Aconite: at the onset of a cold only; Allium cepa: if there is sneezing and watery eyes; Arsenicum: to treat water discharge and dry cough that gets worse at night. Consult a qualified homoeopathic practitioner.

• Supplements – vitamin C and a low dose of a multivitamin and mineral supplement.
• Use Chinese medicine to strengthen the immune system.
• Use a vaporiser to humidify the room especially if you have a dry, blocked nose and cough.
• Bach flower therapy.

# COUGH

According to modern allopathic medicine, coughing is a reflex action to clear the throat of phlegm, mucus, foreign bodies or other irritants. It is caused by irritation due to dust, smoke, gases, or inflammation of the upper airway. A persistent cough may be an indication of an underlying problem and should be investigated. Treatment depends on the cause; in some cases medication is prescribed.

Natural healing methods regard a cough as a way to eliminate irritants. A cough often arises when the energy of the lungs is inadequate or deficient, causing an insufficient elimination of waste. It is also thought that the lungs are weakened by excessive intake of dairy products, which cause an accumulation of mucus in the system.

## Glands
Thyroid, parathyroid and thymus

## Chakras
*Throat* Affirmation – 'I open myself for creative expression and release built-up toxicity'
*Heart* Affirmation – 'I am willing to receive and give love freely'

## Emotional cause

A cough usually indicates that we are trying to release tension in the throat, perhaps to 'get something off our chest'. This can be associated with frustration and an irritating attitude. It could also be an aspect of ourselves that we are not aligned with. Could you be choking on life, not receiving what you need to be at ease in your life?

## Reiki treatment

Use positions 4 and 5. You could treat the liver and throat at the same time: put one hand at the throat and the other hand directly over the area of the liver. You will find the cough will subside almost immediately.

## Recommended complementary treatment

• Eliminate all dairy products from your diet so the body has a better chance to be clear of the mucus that irritates the throat.
• Homoeopathy – Aconite: for a cough that comes from exposure to cold, dry winds; Belladonna: for sudden onset of a dry, teasing cough and red face; Bryonia: for a hard, dry cough that is usually worse when entering into a warm room; Phosphorus: for a dry, tickling cough that comes from a head cold moving down into the chest. Consult a homoeopathic practitioner.
• Acupressure – to support the lung meridian.
• Acupuncture – to stimulate and strengthen the kidneys and the liver.
• Herbal treatment is used both to bring up mucus and also to treat the cough. Consult a herbalist.
• Bach flower therapy.

# HICCUPS

According to modern allopathic medicine, hiccups are an involuntary contraction of the diaphragm (muscle below the ribs) and rapid closure of the vocal chords producing a sharp sound. They are usually only brief in duration. The cause is related to an irritation of nerves in the gastrointestinal tract. Treatment is not normally required. For prolonged bouts of hiccuping medication may be given.

Natural healing methods contend that hiccups are due to an imbalance in the stomach, spleen and diaphragm. Eating a meal too quickly or drinking cold, carbonated drinks that have a shocking and irritating effect on the stomach and spleen can cause this imbalance. Various techniques from the sublime to the ridiculous are used to stop hiccups.

## Glands
Adrenals

## Chakras
*Solar Plexus* Affirmation – 'I breathe through all spasms and remain open to life'

## Emotional cause
It is thought that the emotional cause of hiccups is that we want to take in life too fast. Life is a pleasurable experience that can be enjoyed moment to moment. Do you want to have it all right now?

## Reiki treatment
Use position **6**, placing your hand directly over the diaphragm, which is located below the breastbone. You can also sandwich the body by placing one hand on the back and the other over the diaphragm. Encourage slow, deep breathing.

## Recommended complementary treatment

- Drink ten sips of water in rapid succession.
- Drink a glass of water from the opposite side of the glass.
- Eat a cube of sugar.
- Apply ice to your neck.
- Take a tablespoon of vinegar.
- Have someone scare you.
- Lie on your side for fifteen minutes.
- Stand on your head.

# INFLUENZA (FLU)

According to allopathic medicine, influenza is an infection of the respiratory tract. It is characterised by head and muscle aches, fever and chills. Cold symptoms appear as influenza subsides. It is caused by three main influenza viruses: types A, B and C. Treatment is symptomatic and includes rest, plenty of fluids, paracetamol, nasal decongestants, steam inhalation and throat lozenges. Only in severe cases are antibiotics prescribed.

In natural healing methods flu is not distinguished from the common cold. It is looked upon as the body's way to eliminate stored-up waste and poisons that have accumulated due to poor eating, stress, lack of exercise and inadequate rest. Waste products weaken the immune system and create the foothold needed for the virus to work in the body. Often in allopathic medicine, medication is given to reduce symptoms or to stop the cleansing process, but this actually works against the system as it drives the waste products further into the system. Flu, like the cold, can be looked upon as the body's rapid form of internal cleansing. More rest and fluids need to be taken to support the process of cleansing.

## Glands
Pituitary, thyroid, parathyroid, thymus and adrenals

## Chakras
*Third Eye* Affirmation – 'I open my intuitive process to find what thoughts have blocked me'
*Throat* Affirmation – 'I express all my emotions and release my need to control myself'
*Heart* Affirmation – 'I am open to receiving and giving love. I release any pain that is stored there'
*Solar Plexus* Affirmation – 'I release all toxins, including toxic thoughts and emotions'
*Sacral Centre* Affirmation – 'I am in perfect harmony with all aspects of myself'

## Emotional cause
Have you been doing too much? Have you stressed your body beyond its maximum capabilities? Getting the flu can also indicate that you need time to integrate your life experiences. Where are the emotional issues that need to be released? What thoughts and feelings are you holding on to that weaken your immune system? When will you say yes to yourself even if it means saying no to another person?

## Reiki treatment
Use position **1** to help clear any sinus blockage, position **4** for the throat, position **5** for the upper chest, and positions **6** to **8** for the spleen, liver and colon. Also use position **18** to strengthen the immune system.

## Recommended complementary treatment
• Get plenty of rest, drink plenty of fluids. Keep lighting low and keep warm.

• Respect the demands of your body. This is not a time to push yourself. Use this time to establish a healthy way to support your body, mind and spirit.
• Homoeopathy – Aconite: at the onset of a cold only; Allium cepa: if there is sneezing and watery eyes; Arsenicum: to treat water discharge and dry cough that gets worse at night. Consult a qualified homoeopathic practitioner.
• Supplements – vitamin C and a low dose of a multivitamin and mineral supplement.
• Use Chinese medicine to strengthen the immune system.
• Use a vaporiser to humidify the room especially if you have a dry, blocked nose and cough.
• Bach flower therapy.

## SORE THROAT

According to allopathic medicine, the symptoms of a sore throat are a rough, scratchy feeling in the back of the throat. It is usually a sign of an underlying problem such as inflammation of the pharynx and/or larynx, tonsillitis, common cold, influenza, glandular fever, or childhood diseases such as measles, mumps and chicken pox. Symptoms may be relieved by gargling with salt water and taking aspirin (not children). Prolonged or persistent sore throats should be investigated.

From the viewpoint of natural healing methods, a sore throat results when the body is attempting to eliminate accumulated toxins, especially from the intestinal tract and lymph system. Imbalance in the intestine is the main cause of this complaint.

### Glands
Thyroid, parathyroid, thymus, adrenals and gonads

## Chakras

*Throat* Affirmation – 'I freely communicate all my thoughts and emotions'

*Sacral Centre* Affirmation – 'I release all conflict that holds me back from my inner harmony'

*Root* Affirmation – 'I accept and acknowledge my right to be here'

## Emotional cause

The throat is where we swallow our reality. It is where we take in food and the process of living. We release our emotions through verbal communication using our throat. The throat can become sore and inflamed when we have to swallow a reality that we do not want to, when we repress anger and rage or where there is a conflict in our expression. The throat also represents conception, so difficulties here can also reflect a deep conflict in accepting our right to be here.

## Reiki treatment

Treat the large intestine using positions **6** to **8** the throat with position **4**, and the lymphatic system with positions **19** and **20**.

## Recommended complementary treatment

• Treat with Chinese medicine to strengthen the large intestine and increase elimination.
• Do some journal writing to express and cleanse out your feelings.
• Use meditation to remove stress and worry.
• Take walks out in nature to bring you back into harmony.
• Try singing in groups to open your communication.
• Use group therapy to discuss the emotions and feelings you haven't expressed.
• Bach flower therapy.

# 12
# THE SPECIAL SENSES

**The special senses** are made up of the cells, organs and tissues that give us our sense of smell, taste, vision and hearing. Eyes and ears are the subject of this section.

## THE EYE

**The eye is the organ** of sight. Light waves enter the eye and are transformed into electrical impulses. These impulses travel along nerves into the brain where it interprets them as images.

The eye is a circular, fluid-filled ball held in place, in the bony eye sockets, by groups of muscle tissue. The outer layer is made of a tough white fibrous tissue, except at the very front, called sclera. The cornea is a transparent, fibrous tissue that meets with the ends of the sclera to seal off the eyeball. It acts as the main lens, which focuses light entering the eye. Sitting behind the cornea is a fluid-filled (aqueous humour) chamber that contains the iris. The iris (coloured part of the eye) lies at the rear of this chamber. The iris is made of muscle that expands and contracts, in response to light, varying the size of the pupil. The pupil is the hole through which light enters the eye. The lens sits behind the iris and is connected to a group of muscles called the ciliary body. The ciliary body expands and contracts, altering the shape of the lens, thus allowing light to be further focused as it enters the eye. Behind the lens is another chamber of gel-filled fluid (vitreous humour). The back of the eyeball is made up of complex nerve fibres called the retina. Light waves, which enter through the pupil, focused by the cornea and the lens, converge on the retina. Specialised cells (photoreceptors) called rods and cones in the retina react to light and send a complex set of electrical impulses to the brain via the optic (sight) nerve. The visual centre of the brain then interprets these impulses as images.

# THE EAR

**The ear is the organ** of hearing and balance. Sound vibrations pass through the ear where they are transformed into electrical impulses that travel through nerves into the brain. The brain interprets these impulses as sound. Similarly, information pertaining to balance and posture is transferred from impulses originating in the ear to the brain.

There are three predominant components of the ear: the outer, middle and inner ear. The outer ear comprises the pinna (ear lobe), which collects sound waves and directs them towards the inner ear through the ear canal. At the end of the canal is the eardrum (a skin/tissue membrane) which separates the outer ear from the middle ear. The drum vibrates in response to sound waves sent down the ear canal. This in turn sends vibrations down the bones of the middle ear, the malleus (hammer), incus (anvil) and the stapes (stirrup). Within the middle ear is also the Eustachian (auditory) tube, which passes down the back of the nose. The Eustachian tube responds to changes in air pressure and acts as a drainage system. Vibrations continue to travel into the inner ear where they connect with bony structures, collectively called the labyrinth. The labyrinth has various structures that aid in sound perception and balance. The front part is a shell-like

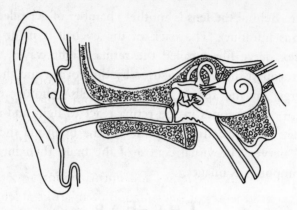

*The ear*

structure called the cochlea, which is involved in sending the vibration on to the acoustic nerve and into the brain, where the vibration is received and interpreted as sound. At the back of the labyrinth are other structures and canals, which are involved with perception of acceleration and gravity. They also receive information regarding position and movement, aiding in balance and posture.

Common conditions of the eye and ear dealt with in this section are cataracts, earache/ear infections, glaucoma, hearing disorders and visual problems.

## CATARACTS

According to modern allopathic medicine, a cataract is a loss of transparency of the lens of the eye. Changes in proteins within the lens are responsible for making it opaque. Advanced cataracts are noticeable by their white, cloudy appearance. Cataracts are the main cause of decreased vision in the elderly. They do not cause complete blindness, but there are marked changes in visual perception due to the restriction of light entering the eye. Severity of visual disturbance depends on the degree of opacity. The cause of cataracts is not known, although it seems to be a normal part of the ageing process. However, congenital cataracts (those present at birth) may be a result of viral infections present in the mother. Cataracts may also result from injury, persistent high blood glucose levels (as in uncontrolled diabetes mellitus) and exposure to forms of radiation such as ultraviolet light and X-rays. Cataract correction is achieved by removal of the affected lens or lenses and normal vision restored by glasses, contact lenses or implantation of an artificial lens.

In natural healing methods, the approach to cataracts is one of prevention, rather than treatment. Alternative therapies for cataracts have not been well proven within or outside the medical profession. It is thought that instances of cataracts increase in areas where people eat a higher amount of fat and protein, and lower levels of beta-carotene and vitamin C. People who have diabetes should look to their diets to prevent the onset of cataracts.

## Glands
Pineal and hypothalamus

## Chakras
*Third Eye* Affirmation – 'I open my insight and look towards a bright future'

## Emotional cause
Losing our sight often implies that there is an inner desire not to see the future. This usually occurs later in life and is connected to the fear of becoming old and helpless. Often the person lives in the past and has nothing to look forward to. In third world countries there is a lack of inner and outer nourishment. From their current perspective the future looks bleak and they cannot imagine it becoming brighter. There

are more cases of cataract among younger people in these countries.

## Reiki treatment
Use positions **1** and **3** to treat the eyes. You can also make a sandwich with one hand on the back of the head and the other over the eyes.

## Recommended complementary treatment
• Foods to use include vegetable juice, especially carrot juice, wholegrains, vegetables high in beta-carotene such as carrots, winter squash, pumpkin, apricots and broccoli.
• Avoid eating animal protein, dairy products, tea, coffee, sugar and alcohol.
• Use creative visualisation, visualising in your mind's eye that you are seeing clearly. Take a look at your life and see all the people around you who love and respect you. Life is happy.
• Chinese medicine will treat the liver meridian, which runs through the eyes, and prescribe foods that stimulate, open and remove stagnation from the liver. Consult a qualified therapist.
• Supplements – beta-carotene: 200 mg per day; vitamin B complex: 50 mg per day; vitamin C: 100 mg per day.
• Bach flower therapy.

# EARACHE AND EAR INFECTIONS

According to allopathic medicine, earache is a pain originating within the ear or its surrounding structures. This is a quite common occurrence in childhood and stems from an infection, but adults are also prone to this problem. Infection can occur in the middle ear (otitis media), ear canal (otitis externa), bone at the rear of the ear (mastoiditis) or inner ear

(labyrinthitis). Rarely, earache is caused through viral infections (e.g. herpes zoster), which produce blisters within the
ear canal. Other forms of earache occur as a result of referred
pain, or pain that occurs in surrounding structures, as in
tonsillitis, throat cancer, and jaw or neck muscle pain.
Persistent build-up of 'glue' in the ear from infection is a
common cause of hearing problems in children. Pain may be
relieved through painkillers. Treatment of earache/infection
depends on the underlying cause; however, medication and
occasionally surgery may be required.

From the viewpoint of natural healing methods, many
chronic or recurrent middle ear infections are actually nutri-
tionally based. A diet rich in mucus-forming foods will bring
about an ear infection.

## Glands
Pituitary, hypothalamus and thyroid

## Chakras
*Third Eye* Affirmation – 'I open my intuition and understand the process'
*Throat* Affirmation – 'I communicate my deepest feelings
and trust the process of life'

## Emotional cause
Ear infections can arise because we do not like what we are
hearing. We are irritated and emotionally upset due to
conflict outside of ourselves. Also our ears will be affected
when we are out of our personal centre and not balanced.

## Reiki treatment
Treat with positions **15** and **16**.

### Recommended complementary treatment
• Eat carrots and carrot juice, citrus fruits, lightly steamed vegetables and rice.
• Avoid eating wheat, dairy products, meat, hydrogenated oils and sugar.
• Homoeopathy – Belladonna: for sudden onset earaches; Chamomile: for children with stuffy ears and pain. Consult a qualified homoeopathic practitioner.
• Tea tree oil is an anti-inflammatory. Massage around the outer ear and neck region.
• Write down in a journal what it is you do not want to hear. This is an excellent way to release what is bothering you. Let your feelings flow on to the paper.

# GLAUCOMA

Modern allopathic medicine states that glaucoma is an abnormal increase in the fluid pressure within the eye (intraocular pressure). Raised intraocular pressure causes constriction and compression of blood vessels in the eyes, particularly those that supply the optic nerve, causing damage. As the optic nerve is responsible for transmitting messages involved in visual perception, any damage to it will result in impaired vision. An increase in intraocular pressure results from an obstructed flow of fluid within the eye; this may be part of the normal ageing process, or come from injury or infection of the eye. Congenital (present at birth) glaucoma results from abnormal structure of the eye. Sudden raised intraocular pressure, resulting in pain in the eye, altered vision, nausea and vomiting, is a medical emergency and requires immediate attention. Glaucoma can be controlled with medication; however surgery may be required to correct fluid flow.

According to natural healing methods, glaucoma is related to stress and a disorder of the liver due to improper diet and lifestyle. It is said that fat is the most damaging food consumed by human beings. The prolonged use of fat and its effects can be measured in nearly every organ in the body. When fat levels are surpassed by diet the liver can become deficient, toxins build up, and the hormone composition of the blood changes. This hormonal change is what causes plaque. Plaque prevents the blood from flowing optimally, thus causing pressure to build up in the eye.

## Glands
Pituitary and thalamus

## Chakras
*Third Eye* Affirmation – 'I forgive old hurts and open to a world of possibility'

## Emotional cause
Sometimes we think that what lies ahead of us is not a pretty sight. Our past experience has caused hurt and/or an opportunity to hold on to long-standing hurts. We have not released pent-up tears. In older age we cannot do as we did when we were younger. We see ourselves becoming slower and more set in our ways. It is emotionally upsetting and difficult to accept what happens as we age. Our distant vision blurs and we can only focus on now. We are unable to see the vastness and expansiveness of life and embrace it.

## Reiki treatment
Positions **1** and **2**.

## Recommended complementary treatment
• When the liver is involved in the disorder eat vegetables, especially leafy greens, carrots, and all other root vegetables.
• Drink vegetable juices, especially carrot juice. Undertake a

three-to-four-day carrot juice fast to cleanse the liver (see page 59).
• Avoid alcohol, coffee, tea and artificially sweetened beverages. Drink gumplant herbal tea.
• Homoeopathy – Gumplant tincture. Consult a qualified homoeopathic practitioner.
• Supplements – beta-carotene, vitamins B1, B2, B6 and E.

# HEARING DISORDERS

According to allopathic medicine, deafness, or total hearing loss, is rare. Total deafness is often congenital (present at birth) resulting from faulty or absent structures of hearing. Partial deafness is more common. It usually stems either from problems associated with sound waves reaching the inner ear (conductive) or the transmission of sound messages along the hearing pathway (sensorineural). In adults the common cause of conductive deafness results from a build-up of 'wax' in the ear which blocks the outer ear canal. In children it results from a build-up of 'glue' due to middle ear infections. Rarely, conductive deafness is due to damage of the eardrum. Sensorineural deafness may result from congenital birth defects through the unborn child being exposed to rubella (German measles), or it may be caused soon after birth as a result of jaundice (build-up of bile in the blood). Damage may also result from excessive exposure to noise, toxicity from some drugs, viral infection or tumour of the acoustic (hearing) nerve. Hearing loss is also a natural part of ageing. Treatment varies from clearing obstructions (glue, wax) to surgical intervention to repair some types of ear damage. However, not all causes of deafness can be reversed. In these cases other options are considered, that is hearing aids, hearing implants, lip-reading and sign language.

Those who follow natural healing methods view loss of hearing as a problem with circulation of blood, lymph and energy in the inner ear. When the blood and lymph cannot circulate freely in the inner ear, oxygen and immune cells cannot reach the cells to nourish them and the result is that they can become deformed. Hearing problems are related to kidney imbalance.

## Glands
Pineal, hypothalamus, thyroid and adrenals

## Chakras
*Third Eye* Affirmation – 'Life is joyously received and integrated'
*Throat* Affirmation – 'I trust that what I hear supports my life process'
*Solar Plexus* Affirmation – 'I am open to change and go with the flow of life'

## Emotional cause
What do you not want to take in from the outside any more? Are you living in a home with a lot of fighting and disharmony, or do you work in an environment that is full of discord so that you retreat into your own world? Do you not want to deal with or accept what you are hearing?

## Reiki treatment
Treat the ears using positions **15** and **16**. Also treat the kidneys using positions **12** and **13**.

## Recommended complementary treatment
• Avoid eating refined sugar, synthetic ingredients, carbonated drinks and dairy products that create excessive amounts of mucus.

• Avoid foods that will tax the kidneys such as foods high in salt.
• Consult a dietician to recommend foods to strengthen the kidneys.
• Consult a herbalist to recommend kidney-strengthening herbs.
• Acupressure will strengthen the kidney meridian.
• Change your location away from disharmony and fighting if possible.

# VISION PROBLEMS

According to allopathic medicine, the most common form of vision disorder is related to the refraction or bending of light as it passes through the lens of the eye. Myopia (short-sight) occurs when distant images are focused in front of the retina. Thus, distant objects are blurry and near objects are clear. Hypermetropia (long-sight) occurs when distant objects are focused on the retina but close objects focus past the retina, which results in distant objects being viewed as normal but near objects being blurry. Presbyopia is a failure of the ciliary body to alter the shape of the lens to focus images. Astigmatism occurs when the cornea (transparent lining of the front of the eye) is abnormally shaped, resulting in blurring of images. Glasses or contact lenses can correct all visual abnormalities relating to an alteration in the refraction of light. Other visual abnormalities may result from over- or underdeveloped muscles (squint or strabismus) or an alteration in the visual pathway, that is, resulting from disorders of the optic nerve and visual centre of the brain.

Natural healing methods maintain that the liver nourishes the eyes. When the liver meridian has less energy, distortion begins to occur. All forms of eye disorder therefore are seen as stemming from liver imbalance.

## Glands
Pituitary and adrenals

## Chakras
*Third Eye* Affirmation – 'I see the beauty of life around me'
*Solar Plexus* Affirmation – 'My inner reality and my outer reality nourish me'

## Emotional cause
The eyes express every emotion and feeling being experienced inwardly. How the eye functions reflects how we see life and our relationship to whatever is occurring, as follows:

**Near-sightedness** means focusing on the immediate reality and not wanting to look ahead to the future.

**Far-sightedness** usually indicates ignoring the personal and present in favour of dreaming about the future. This person is normally extrovert and gregarious.

**Astigmatism** is related to strong parental influence where fear and abuse cause the child to see the world in a different way.

**Eyestrain** indicates trying too hard to find the answers outside of ourselves.

**Blindness** indicates withdrawal so that we are protected from having to deal with a reality that is too much to cope with.

**Blurred vision** shows our reality is not the same as that of others.

**Wide or bulging eyes** are eyes that are in a constant state of shock. This is usually developed in childhood.

**Itchy eyes** indicate that something we are seeing is causing us irritation.

## Reiki treatment
Use positions 1 and 3 for visual problems, and positions 6 and 7 to treat the liver.

## Recommended complementary treatment
• Get plenty of rest and exercise.
• Use Chinese medicine to strengthen the liver.
• Consult a Bates eye practitioner to teach you exercises to strengthen the eyes.
• Consult a qualified homoeopathic practitioner for a constitutional treatment.

# 13

# THE URINARY SYSTEM

**The urinary system** of the body comprises the kidneys, renal pelvis, ureter, bladder and urethra. The urinary system is responsible for the formation and excretion of urine. The kidneys are located either side of the body at the base of the ribs. Kidneys filter the blood and excrete excess water and waste products from the body. The renal pelvis connects the kidneys to the ureter, a long tube that drains urine into the bladder. The bladder is a muscular sac, located within the pelvis, that stores urine until it can be emptied via the urethra, a tube that runs to the outside of the body and is located in the penis in men and just in front of the vagina in women. As the bladder expands it sends messages to the brain which signals the urethral sphincter muscle (in the neck of the bladder) to relax and allow urine to flow out of the urethra.

Common conditions of the urinary system dealt with in this section include bladder problems such as cystitis, enuresis (bed-wetting) and incontinence.

## BLADDER PROBLEMS

According to modern allopathic medicine, symptoms of bladder problems often include incontinence of various types: there is a stress variety that includes the release of a small amount of urine when laughing, sneezing, coughing or exer-

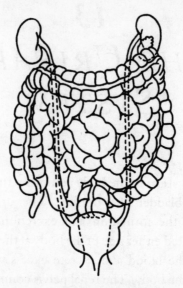

*The urinary system*

cising; the overflow variety, which is the inability to fully empty the bladder when urinating and there may be leaking during the day; the urge variety that is triggered by the sound of running water; and, the reflex variety, which is the emptying of the bladder without having felt the need to urinate beforehand. Bladder problems also include swelling of the bladder or urethra and a weakness or over-activity of the sphincter muscles. These conditions can be produced by over-active or under-active bladder muscles, neurological disorders, hormone imbalance and the side-effects of medication.

Other bladder problems can result from tumours, stones (calculi), injury and nerve degeneration. Treatment will vary according to the specific cause.

Those who follow natural healing methods describe bladder problems as representing an imbalance of the energy which is usually brought on by eating highly acidic foods and drinks. Other irritants that stress the bladder and kidneys include intra-uterine birth control devices and cigarette smoking.

## Glands
Adrenals and gonads

## Chakras
*Sacral Centre* Affirmation – 'I accept myself as a sexual person, I honour the pursuit of my life passions'
*Root* Affirmation – 'I have stability, I am being here and in the now moment'

## Emotional cause
It is thought that bladder problems stem emotionally from anxiety. Life is supporting us to let go of old ideas that no longer serve us, yet we have a fear of fully letting go. It also can be about being totally disgusted with ourselves or others.

## Reiki treatment
Use positions **9** and **29** to treat bladder and urinary tract problems.

## Recommended complementary treatment
• Practise Kegal exercises to strengthen the bladder muscles. Contract the pelvic muscles several times a day using a rhythmic contraction, release and contraction again. This will strengthen the sphincter muscles in the bladder.
• Walk daily and do aerobic exercise.
• Avoid eating highly acidic foods such as spices, alcohol, sugar, tomatoes, hot peppers, red meat, dairy products, eggs, excess salt, and products containing caffeine such as coffee, tea and cocoa (these act as diuretics and will weaken the bladder wall).
• Drink herbal teas. Burdock root strengthens the kidneys

and bladder, and cleanses the blood. Buchu is recommended for cystitis (inflammation of the bladder), irritation of the urethra, high levels of uric acid and urine retention. Take teas three to four times a day.

# CYSTITIS AND URETHRITIS

According to allopathic medicine, the main symptoms of these inflammatory conditions are frequent urination accompanied by a burning sensation, with pain in the bladder area. Even if the bladder is empty there may be an intense desire to pass urine. The urine may be cloudy and have a strong odour. Cystitis is usually caused by bacterial growth on the bladder wall. The condition is common in women because of the short (4–5 cm) urethral opening, giving external bacteria a short passageway to the bladder. In men cystitis usually occurs because of urine retention secondary to bladder or urethral obstruction. Consuming large quantities of water will help flush out the infection. Medication may also be prescribed.

Natural healing methods recognise that bacteria may be present in the bladder, however that is not the real cause of the disease. It is believed that the sufferer's immune system is not in harmony due to improper diet, not enough exercise and a lifestyle not supporting the body (being too busy to pay proper attention to taking care of the body).

## Glands
Adrenals and gonads

## Chakras
*Sacral Centre* Affirmation – 'I open myself to the healthy expression of my passion'
*Root* Affirmation – 'I am centred and walk to the beat of my own drum'

## Emotional cause

Emotions can accumulate and cause the bladder to become irritated and inflamed. It is in the urine that we release all our unwanted and negative emotions. Emotions that are held on to become an irritant if we do not release them. The bladder is in the pelvic area. We give birth to ourselves and our freedom from dependency comes from this area. Often these illnesses may indicate relationship problems, especially with a partner.

## Reiki treatment

Use position 9 and 29.

## Recommended complementary treatment

• Eat foods that support the immune system as well as help to clear infection: salads, wholegrains, lightly cooked vegetables high in protein (such as peas, beans and lentils), fish containing fatty acids, cranberry juice, carrots, lemon juice, eight glasses of pure spring water daily, Buchu tea and fresh fruit.
• Avoid eating meat, dairy products, eggs, citrus fruit, refined sugar, oily foods, salt, caffeine, alcohol and spicy foods.
• Practise Kegal exercises (see 'Bladder problems', p. 187) to strengthen the bladder, and abdominal exercises to restore strength and control to the pelvic floor.
• Meditate to restore harmony and give insight as to what thoughts need to be released.

# ENURESIS (BED-WETTING)

According to allopathic medicine, enuresis is the medical term for bed-wetting. This most commonly occurs in children and is due to slow maturation of the nerves involved in bladder control. Psychological stress may also be a factor to be considered. Other causes of enuresis include diabetes mellitus, urinary tract infections, nervous system defects (e.g. spina bifida, spinal damage) or poor bladder control. Treatment depends on the cause. It may include treating underlying problems, bladder control training, use of night alarms that awake a person the moment urine is passed and, in some circumstances, medication.

Those who follow natural healing methods believe that eating excessive sugar and drinking too many soft drinks can expand the bladder or weaken control over it. Excessively cold conditions can cause frequent urination in children. Bed-wetting can also have psychological causes related to fear of school, a new baby in the house or problems experienced with the break-up of the family. Spinal lesions due to trauma at birth or a fall can also induce problems and a spinal examination is recommended.

## Glands
Adrenals and gonads

## Chakras
*Solar Plexus* Affirmation – 'I fully express my concerns and fears'
*Sacral Centre* Affirmation – 'I am open and responsive to all aspects of my being'
*Root* Affirmation – 'I feel fully supported by life'

## Emotional cause
Bed-wetting is an uncontrollable and unconscious release of negative emotion that may be caused by a feeling of rejection, being unworthy or insecurity about the future. Because the release is at night when the child is asleep it indicates that the conflict is deep and on an unconscious level. Blaming the child will only create further conflict and inner pain.

## Reiki treatment

Treat the bladder, pancreas and kidneys with positions **7**, **12**, **13** and **29**.

## Recommended complementary treatment

• Eat small amounts of Nori seaweed to increase mineral levels, and strengthen the bladder and kidneys, white fish and black beans.

• Avoid soft drinks, sugar, strong spices and non-organic foods that may contain pesticides.

• Homoeopathy – Belladonna: for the child who sleeps so soundly he cannot wake up, or is sensitive to cold and changes in the weather; Causticum: for the child who wets in the first few hours of sleep; Equisetum: for the child who has nightmares and the fear triggers the release; Pulsatilla: for the child who is shy and sensitive. Consult a qualified homoeopathic practitioner.

• Use Chinese medicine to strengthen the kidneys.

• Supplements – beta-carotene: 15–30 mg per day; vitamin B complex: 25 mg per day; vitamin E: 100–200 IU, once per day.

• Massage over the kidney area with olive oil to strengthen the kidneys.

• Bach flower therapy.

# INCONTINENCE

According to allopathic medicine, incontinence is the inability to control the flow of urine from the bladder. Causes range from obstruction of the bladder and/or urethra to total loss of bladder and sphincter muscle control, resulting in overflow of urine or complete uncontrolled emptying of the bladder. Incontinence is often classified as stress incontinence, urge incontinence, total incontinence and overflow incontinence. It has been known to occur after childbirth.

Treatment ranges from pelvic muscle exercises, to medication and self-catheterisation.

Natural healing methods state that bladder problems leading to incontinence will arise from weakened energy to the kidneys. Several other problems can pertain to incontinence such as urinary tract infections, constipation, muscle and sphincter weakness, hormonal problems, neurological disorders and being overweight. Treatment is designed to promote increased energy to the kidneys and to strengthen the muscles that promote a healthy bladder.

## Glands
Adrenals and gonads

## Chakras
*Solar Plexus* Affirmation – 'My emotional and mental life is harmonised. I am open and respond from the Yes in me'
*Root* Affirmation – 'I am supported and fully in control of what happens in my life'

## Emotional cause
Weakened muscle control can also be seen as a weakened emotional and mental attitude. We may feel that we have lost control of what is happening to us in our lives. Our inner fears, feelings, anxiety and concerns have changed and we find that we are less able to deal with them. It is essential for us to reassure, accept and love ourselves.

## Reiki treatment
Treat the bladder using positions **9** and **29**. Treat the kidneys using positions **12** and **13**.

## Recommended complementary treatment
• Avoid eating products containing caffeine, alcohol, sugar,

acidic juices, spicy foods, milk products, tobacco, cocoa and carbonated drinks.

• Kegel exercises will strengthen the muscles of the bladder (see 'Bladder Problems', p. 187).

• Have an acupressure or acupuncture treatment to strengthen the kidney meridian.

# 14
# MULTI SYSTEM DISORDERS

**Throughout the rest of** this part of the book ailments have been classified, and explored, according to the primary body system that is affected. While it can be said that all ailments do indeed affect more than one system, the choice to classify them under a particular system was made by way of reflecting various specialised functions of individual body systems.

The ailments that follow have been classified in this multi system section as no primary system is involved: anxiety, depression, dizziness, fatigue, headaches, heatstroke, hyperactivity, insomnia, memory disturbances, migraines and stress.

## ANXIETY

According to allopathic medicine, anxiety is a condition in which a person has a heightened sense of emotional arousal (awareness) in relation to fear or concern, for example. A person may experience anxiety on a broad spectrum from mild unease to an intense, debilitating fear. Theories describing the cause of anxiety vary, including physiological (an increased arousal of the central nervous system), psychoanalytical (stemming from a fear of loss or unconscious conflict) and behavioural (a learned response). A multitude of systemic responses produce various symptoms, in varying degrees, including palpitations, chest pain, alterations in breathing, muscle spasm and pain, nausea, loss of appetite, diarrhoea, sweating, dizziness, light-headedness, irrational fears, feelings of doom, frequency of urination, excessive worry, irritability, fatigue, restlessness and/or sleep disturbances. Treatment approaches include counselling, psychotherapy or medication.

Those who follow natural healing methods view a certain amount of anxiety as normal and part of living life. Healthy anxiety can aid you in dealing with situations that cause you stress. When anxiety becomes excessive it needs to be treated. High levels of anxiety are caused by an imbalance of the spleen, pancreas and stomach. Normally these organs become imbalanced due to large amounts of sugar, acid-rich food or excess thinking (i.e. mulling things over). Anxiety causes premature ageing, muscle tension, and weakness of the immune system and the kidneys. A person experiencing anxiety may have a tight or acid stomach, rapid breathing, sweating, headache, nausea, difficulty in swallowing, hoarseness, weight loss over a prolonged time and sexual impotence.

## Glands
Pineal, hypothalamus and adrenals

## Chakras
*Crown* Affirmation – 'I am open to life and its infinite flow'
*Solar Plexus* Affirmation – 'I am willing to redefine myself and know I am not alone in this world'

## Emotional cause
Anxiety is seen as a separation from oneness or the source of life. This separation happens when we get so focused on doing 'it' ourselves and we fail to remember that God, or what we hold as that Creative Essence, also sources us.

Anxiety heightens as we put ourselves first, squeezing all the joy out of life in favour of money or position etc., disconnecting ourselves from our Divine Source. Life may seem overwhelming. We feel, fear and think that we are alone. A healthy amount of anxiety is what motivates humans to search for life's answers and mysteries. It is what enables people to establish greater faith.

## Reiki treatment
Treat the crown using position **2**, and the solar plexus area, especially the spleen, pancreas and stomach, using positions **6** to **8**. On the back treat the kidneys and adrenal glands using positions **11** to **13**.

## Recommended complementary treatment
• Avoid foods that produce acid and increase nervous tension such as sugar, soft drinks, coffee and tea.
• Take regular daily exercise. Walk and take deep, relaxing breaths to slow your mind down.
• Meditate twice a day, surrendering yourself to God or whatever you hold as the Creative Essence.
• Massage.
• Let go of any excessive need to control situations, remembering you are part of the whole.
• Bach flower therapy.

# DEPRESSION

According to allopathic medicine, depression is a condition in which a person experiences feelings of sadness, hopelessness and a generalised loss of interest in life. Depression may be experienced to differing levels of severity. Persistent, deep depression affecting behaviour and well-being is often an indication of an underlying psychiatric illness. A person with depression may exhibit any of the following characteristics: mood fluctuations, anxiety, bouts of crying, loss of appetite, sleep disturbances, withdrawal from social interaction, tiredness and/or poor concentration. Profound depression may be marked by inclinations towards suicide, self-harm and/or altered perception. Theories about depression include biological (viral infection, hormonal changes, response to medications) and psychological (responses to various life events, e.g. parental relationships, losses) causes. Treatment is dependent on underlying causes and includes psychotherapy and medication.

Those who follow natural healing methods view depression as the result of inadequate levels of serotonin, which occurs naturally in the body and is responsible for feelings of well-being and restful sleep. Serotonin is increased in the brain by high consumption of carbohydrates, increased exercise and decreased hours of sleeping to a maximum of six hours per night.

## Glands
Pineal, hypothalamus, thymus and adrenals

## Chakras
*Crown* Affirmation – 'I open myself to accept other forms of support'
*Third Eye* Affirmation – 'I see that I am not alone and can rest in this knowledge'
*Heart* Affirmation – 'I forgive all others and myself for what I have held on to as wrong and unjust'
*Solar Plexus* Affirmation – 'I reclaim my personal power'

## Emotional cause
Depression involves a deep inner sadness that life is not as we wish it to be. Our reality is not the same as life's reality, and

thus we become fragmented in body and mind. Have you lost your purpose and meaning for living? Have you given up on yourself?

## Reiki treatment

Treat the head, heart and solar plexus. The depressed person has become fragmented in their body and mind, thus cutting off the creative essence. This also leads to a feeling of being alone. Therefore use positions **1** and **2** for the head, **6** to **8** for the solar plexus, and **23** for the heart.

## Recommended complementary treatment

• Journal writing for twenty to thirty minutes a day to express your feelings. This is not for re-reading; rather this exercise serves as a way to get those feelings out that have been held on to for so long.

• Sleep management – if you are sleeping in excess of eight hours per day it can be helpful to reduce this amount to about six hours because often people will sleep to avoid confronting problems when they are depressed. On the other hand, if you sleep less than six hours per night increase the amount of hours you sleep to between six and seven hours.

• Meditate daily using creative visualisation to see yourself happy and fulfilled in life with many friends around you.

• Support groups – join a group of people who are positive and uplifting for support.

• Do some community service. Often when we focus on others our own problems seem smaller.

• Take a daily walk to increase oxygen in the blood and take yourself out into the world.

• Any aerobic exercise like cycling or swimming will be helpful.

• Bach flower therapy.

# DIZZINESS

According to allopathic medicine, dizziness is a momentary feeling of unsteadiness or light-headedness. Causes of dizziness vary: a change in the blood pressure of the brain; as a result of medication; low blood pressure; blockages of arteries; tiredness; stress; fever; anaemia; low blood glucose levels; and bleeding within the brain. Dizziness can also be experienced as part of a more specific condition called vertigo, in which a person feels like they are spinning. This is accompanied by nausea, vomiting, sweating and/or fainting. Vertigo can indicate an underlying inner ear problem or disturbances of the acoustic (hearing) nerve. Brief episodes of dizziness usually pass requiring no treatment, but persistent dizziness or vertigo should be investigated. Treatment will vary according to the identified cause; often medication may be prescribed.

In natural healing methods it is suggested that dizziness is brought about because there is an imbalance in the liver meridian causing loss of equilibrium.

## Glands
Hypothalamus, thyroid, thalamus and pituitary

## Chakras
*Third Eye* Affirmation – 'I am inspired by higher sources'
*Throat* Affirmation – 'I open and communicate my needs and desires'
*Heart* Affirmation – 'I receive all that is needed to nurture me'

## Emotional cause
Dizziness represents a loss of balance. We have moved out of our centre, and lost our stability and our sense of being grounded.

## Reiki treatment

Use the blood pressure treatment position **17** and treat the heart using position **23**.

## Recommended complementary treatment

• Ensure you get plenty of sleep to keep the liver calm.

• Eat foods to stimulate the liver to overcome dizziness, such as sauerkraut, black pepper, ginger, dill, cumin, basil, honey mixed with lemon, cucumber, onions and watercress.

• Drink vegetable juices.

• Use creative visualisation and meditation to see what it is you want to run from and visualise that you are whole and happy as you are.

# FATIGUE

According to allopathic medicine, fatigue is a general feeling of tiredness, often characterised by lack of energy, drowsiness, decreased motivation, lack of vitality and feelings of exhaustion. Fatigue on its own is commonly a result of lack of sleep or poor diet. Persistent episodes of fatigue, accompanied by other symptoms, should be investigated. It may be an indication of an underlying condition such as sleep disorders, anaemia, cancer, depression or anxiety. Treatment of fatigue on its own consists of rest, sleep and dietary changes.

According to natural healing methods, in the everyday hustle and bustle of life people seem to push themselves to extremes. We take inadequate exercise and do not allow a few moments just to turn off the mind from the problems and events of the day. We also do not sleep enough. Fatigue is a modern ailment that affects most people. Our lives are lived without harmony. We prefer work to play; we forget intimacy, spiritual practice and rest. Over time, living in this state will create increasing tension in our emotions, mind and

# COMMON AILMENTS

body. This tension will also slow down vital energy in the body. Individual organs become fatigued and the accumulation of toxins takes place. Fatigue should be considered as the body's way of speaking to us, telling us we are out of balance and asking us to make corrections in our style of living, so that vitality can return and become our normal and natural state.

## Glands
Adrenals

## Chakras
*Solar Plexus* Affirmation – 'I hear my body's message and take the time to come into harmony'
*Sacral Centre* Affirmation – 'I honour my body's need to be expressive, playful and sensual'

## Emotional cause
Fatigue indicates a loss of purpose and a need to reconnect to your inner joy and love of life. You have over-depleted yourself mentally and/or physically. Your reserves are all used up and you may be weary of coping with life and all that you have undertaken.

## Reiki treatment
Use the immune system stimulation position **18**; also use positions **7**, **8**, **12** and **13**.

## Recommended complementary treatment
• Eat foods that are rich in iron, folic acid and vitamin B12.
• Get enough sleep every night: aim for seven to eight hours.
• Walk at least three times a week for half-an-hour. Try to walk in nature to enable you to be nourished by your environment and to calm the mind.

201

- Multivitamin and mineral supplements.
- Massage with aromatherapy oils to stimulate the body and for relaxation. Shiatsu massages are also beneficial.
- Homoeopathy – Arnica: for fatigue from overwork; Arsenicum: for anxiety. Consult a qualified homoeopathic practitioner.
- Use Chinese medicine to strengthen the spleen and pancreas meridians. Also consult your practitioner about foods to warm the body.
- Use meditation for slowing down and releasing tension.
- Play – do what you would like to do but have put off. Allow your inner child to source you. Laughter and play are great healers. Set aside at least thirty minutes a day for this.
- Bach flower therapy.

# HEADACHES

According to allopathic medicine, a headache is experienced as a dull, sharp, throbbing or deep pain in the head. It occurs as a result of constriction, or tension, in the lining of the brain or vessels and muscles of the scalp. Headaches are usually transient and pass with time. Rarely, they are an indication of an underlying serious problem, for example, tumours or high blood pressure. There are varying types, degrees and causes of headaches. Most are simply a result of dietary habits, environmental factors, poor posture, stress or muscle tension. Persistent headaches should be investigated. Treatment options include dietary changes, medication, removing causative factors such as decreasing stresses, improving posture and massage.

Natural healing methods state that a headache is the body's way of communicating the fact that there is an imbalance in our lives causing an adverse effect on our body. Rather than treating the pain of the headache, it is important to seek out the cause of the pain. In most cases this can be traced back to the liver, intestines, poor circulation, stress, menstrual disorders, hypoglycaemia, and pelvic and low back tension.

## Glands
Thyroid, parathyroid, adrenals and gonads

## Chakras
*Throat* Affirmation – 'I release all fear. I trust in the process of life'
*Solar Plexus* Affirmation – 'I release my need to control and go with the flow of life'
*Sacral Centre* Affirmation – 'I am open to life creating with me and through me'

## Emotional cause
A headache is the silent cry of the overburdened mind. We may be stressed or tense. We may be anxious or striving too hard, thus creating a life of tension. Headaches can also occur when we become obsessed with getting ahead. The words you may find yourself using are 'I must, I have, I will'. You have cut off the creative force and are doing it your way. Suppression of thoughts and feelings creates a headache as the reflex effect of negative emotions such as worry or anger. Emotions constrict the blood vessels and cause pain. These emotions can be self-doubt, being over-critical of ourselves, feeling boxed in and trapped in a situation we cannot find a way out of.

## Reiki treatment
Treat the liver, spleen and stomach using positions **6** to **9**. Treat the kidneys with positions **12** and **13**, then the head with positions **1** and **2**. Many headaches respond to treatment on the kidneys.

## Recommended complementary treatment
• Meditate to relax and remove stress.
• Take a walk in nature to get back in touch with the beauty in life.
• Use deep tissue massage to release deep tension.
• Say prayers. Chant.
• Take time out to see things from a different perspective and to stop driving yourself. Find ways to re-establish your inner balance.
• Bowen therapy will open energy in the body.
• Bach flower therapy.

# HEATSTROKE

According to allopathic medicine, heatstroke is a potentially life-threatening condition in which the body's temperature reaches extreme levels. It occurs when the body is exposed to extreme heat and its normal mechanisms of temperature regulation are impeded. This is related to skin and sweat gland disorders, or a response to some medication or environments where temperature and humidity (level of water in the air) are high. Hot, dry, reddened skin, shallow breathing, a weak, racing pulse and cessation of sweating characterise heatstroke. Without arresting the rising temperature a person will collapse into a coma and die. Removing the person's clothing and covering them in a lightweight sheet, which should be kept constantly wet with cold water, will treat heatstroke. A fanning motion can be used to help cool the body. If a person is conscious, they should be given salt water (1/2 teaspoon of salt to a litre of water) or Gatorade, if available, to sip to rehydrate the body.

Those who follow natural healing methods view heatstroke as a life-threatening condition resulting from overexposure to extreme heat. The body's heat-regulating mechanism has broken down and the body temperature becomes dangerously high. Usually a person has been in the sun for a prolonged amount of time and in humid conditions so that the body's natural cooling mechanism of sweating is not activated. Some people are more at risk of heatstroke than others. These include people who spend time on the water sailing or boating, older people in poor health, and those unaccustomed to being in the heat and dressed too warmly.

## Glands
Pineal and adrenals

## Chakras
*Crown* Affirmation – 'I am open to receive support and nourishment from higher sources'
*Solar Plexus* Affirmation – 'I go with the flow of life and am supported to be in the moment'

## Emotional cause
Heatstroke occurs when you are not being mindful of what your body needs. You have possibly allowed someone else to be responsible for you. Take the time to feel your body's comfort. Are you thirsty, do you need to be in the shade? Will you care for yourself?

## Reiki treatment
Use position **30** for treatment of shock.

## Recommended complementary treatment
• As a preventive measure take salt tablets before going out in the sun.

# HYPERACTIVE CHILDREN

According to allopathic medicine, hyperactivity, also known as attention deficit disorder (ADD), is a condition in which predominantly children exhibit poor concentration and excessive activity. Causes of ADD are speculated about and have been theorised to be either hereditary, dietary allergy or mild damage to the brain. Children with ADD are often full of energy, irritable, aggressive, impulsive, emotionally immature and/or have short attention spans, and ADD often affects a child's learning. ADD is treated with stimulant medication, diet, counselling and educational support.

Naturopathy is a natural healing method that treats hyperactivity by removing all refined foods and artificial ingredients from the diet. The child is placed on a totally organic diet, and sugar, wheat, vinegar and dairy products are eliminated. Physical exercise is also recommended as a way for toxins to leave the body naturally.

## Glands
Pineal, hypothalamus and adrenals

## Chakras
*Crown* Affirmation – 'I am fully supported and sourced by a higher energy'
*Third Eye* Affirmation – 'I see possibilities for living my life in harmony'
*Solar Plexus* Affirmation – 'I have inner strength and acceptance. I love myself'

## Emotional cause
Does the child have a fear of failure, or of not being accepted as they are, or paid attention to? Often the parents will give sweets instead of a hug. The child begins to spin out of control,

becoming self-obsessed and not wanting to pay attention to what is outside him. It is the child's cry for time, to be loved and paid attention to with positive reinforcement.

## Reiki treatment
Use positions 1 and 2 to work with the brain, and positions 6 and 7 to work with the liver and pancreas.

## Recommended complementary treatment
• Avoid eating sugar, dairy products, wheat, vinegar, processed food, frozen or canned food and yeast.
• Martial arts such as karate or aikido are useful as they are focused training.
• Massage, especially around the spinal column, to release energy.
• Chamomile tea three times a day.

# INSOMNIA

According to allopathic medicine, insomnia is a disturbance in regular sleep patterns. Insomniacs find it hard to fall asleep or to remain asleep. Symptoms include daytime fatigue, irritability and difficulty in coping. Most adults experience some degree of insomnia, usually caused by excessive worry about daily or future events. However, excessive periods of insomnia may be an indication of an underlying problem such as sleep apnea (periods where breathing stops in sleep), psychiatric illness (anxiety, depression) or drug withdrawal. It may also be related to environmental (noise, light) or lifestyle (too much caffeine, little exercise, irregular hours) factors. Physical causes of insomnia should be investigated. For most people, establishing regular patterns of sleep, work and exercise can aid in developing regular sleeping patterns. Drugs to aid sleep should be avoided.

According to natural healing methods, insomnia is the result of an imbalance in the gallbladder and liver. This is especially true when a person has trouble sleeping between 11 p.m. to 3 a.m., when the body is channelling the energy to these two organs. An excess of other foods and drinks consumed during the day can also be the cause, especially too much coffee, tea, chocolate and soft drinks.

## Glands
Pituitary, pineal, thalamus, hypothalamus and adrenals

## Chakras
*Crown* Affirmation – 'I am safe in the knowledge that I am not alone'
*Third Eye* Affirmation – 'I trust my intuition and accept the beauty of my thoughts and dreams'
*Solar Plexus* Affirmation – 'I open myself to integrate all aspects of my being'

## Emotional cause
Falling asleep is an act of trust. In order to trust you must let go of all activity and control, to open to the unknown. When we sleep we are in a vulnerable and surrendered state. The lack of ability to surrender indicates chronic tension, fear and anxiety. We feel deeply that our ego and survival are being threatened in some way, especially if we have experienced some deep trauma. Insomnia is also linked to the ability to love ourselves, to trust love and therefore to trust life.

## Reiki treatment
Treat the liver and gallbladder using positions 6 and 7. Use positions 1 and 2 to treat the head.

## Recommended complementary treatment
• Eat chlorophyll-rich foods, wholegrains, mushrooms of all types, fruit, seeds, dill and basil.
• Avoid coffee, tea, spicy foods, cola, chocolate and sugar.
• Herbal tea such as rosehip, which contains vitamin C, helps to soothe the nerves.
• Homoeopathy – Nux vomica: when you cannot sleep after a mental strain; Arsenicum: when you cannot sleep because of worry or anxiety; Pulsatilla: for sleeplessness from recurring thoughts. Consult a qualified homoeopathic practitioner.
• Take exercise and fresh air daily. Establish a routine of walking in nature.
• Bach flower therapy.

# MEMORY DISTURBANCES

According to allopathic medicine, memory is the ability to register, store and recall information. Information is first registered and then stored in the short-term memory. Important information is retained in the long-term memory as images, words or sensual associations. Recall, the final stage in memory, is the retrieval of information that has been stored unconsciously. Retrieval depends on how well the information was stored in the long-term memory. The precise mechanism of memory is not known. Memory disturbances can occur at any of the three stages of memory. Predominant problems occur at the recall and retention stage. This is often associated with amnesia (inability to store or recall information in the long-term memory). Registration of information is often affected by conditions like mania (psychological disorder involving excessive activity or irritability) or depression. This is mostly related to the fact that people with these conditions are frequently preoccupied with thoughts rather than being attentive to what needs to be learned. Memory often decreases as a normal process of ageing. Various techniques can be used to aid in the process of retention and recall. However, little can be done to reverse permanent memory loss.

Natural healing methods take the view that this problem arises when the heart and liver are not balanced. The functions of the specific parts of the brain that govern memory are dependent on a balanced heart and liver. The liver is associated with all mental activity, especially study and the retention of ideas and events. The heart as the seat of the spirit is responsible for supporting the memory of important life events. The heart is considered the centre of mental and emotional consciousness, and is related to the nervous system and brain.

## Glands
Pituitary, pineal, thalamus, hypothalamus and adrenals

## Chakras
**Crown** Affirmation – 'I accept and am nourished by a higher form of energy and support'
**Third Eye** Affirmation – 'I accept my intuition is guiding me to my right direction'
**Heart** Affirmation – 'I release all things that would keep me from responding to life and its majesty'
**Solar Plexus** Affirmation – 'I am full of grace and understand in the depth of my being'

## Emotional cause
The head represents our relationship to the abstract as well as being the focal point of experiencing our reality. If we are confused, perhaps we are taking too much on board and cannot sort through all the mental concepts that we are holding on to. Confusion is also a way to withdraw for

a moment. There can also be thought patterns or emotions that are stuck and not going anywhere. Often the outside world will reflect the state of our mind. When we are less centred and confused our home may look messy and untidy.

### Reiki treatment
Treat the heart, liver and head with positions **1**, **2**, **7** and **23**.

### Recommended complementary treatment
• Use Chinese medicine to strengthen the liver, kidney and heart meridians.
• Aerobic exercise will increase oxygen levels to the body.
• Bach flower therapy.

# MIGRAINE HEADACHES

According to allopathic medicine, migraine is a severe form of headache. Nausea, vomiting, visual disturbances and/or stomach complaints often accompany migraines. They tend to be recurrent and can be debilitating. Stress, food sensitivity, bright lights or loud noises may cause them. Menstruation or oral contraceptives may also trigger migraines. Classical migraines have been characterised as beginning with a visual disturbance that subsides and is then followed by a one-sided headache accompanied by nausea, vomiting and sensitivity to light. Sometimes there is also muscle weakness. Common migraines may slowly develop into a throbbing pain in one or both sides of the head, and are often accompanied by nausea and sometimes vomiting. Infrequent migraines are usually treated symptomatically with painkillers and avoidance of potential triggers. Frequent migraines may require more active prevention methods with medication.

Natural healing methods view migraine as a problem that includes sensitivity to light, which indicates an imbalance between the liver and the gallbladder. The liver and gallbladder support the spleen, so if there is an imbalance the spleen will be affected. The spleen is responsible for digestion and if not in harmony could cause nausea. This is a vicious circle of imbalance. Food sensitivity causes a restricted flow of blood and oxygen to the brain, which in turn causes the first stage of the migraine, visual impairment.

## Glands
Pineal, thyroid, parathyroid and adrenals

## Chakras
**Third Eye** Affirmation – 'I look at what needs to be done and have faith in myself and my abilities'
**Throat** Affirmation – 'I trust the process of life and know I can express all my emotions'
**Solar Plexus** Affirmation – 'I am centred. I know I am capable of doing whatever must be done in this moment'

## Emotional cause
When we have a migraine we do not have to deal with what has to be done. We have effectively retreated from life's demands on us. Suppressed rage and an overload of information without the ability to integrate it can also trigger migraines. Our minds may be filled with the endless list of things that need to be done and yet we want to avoid accomplishing this. It has become too much. Is it that you feel you cannot live up to others' expectations and demands? Or do you need unconditional love in this moment?

## Reiki treatment
Treat the spleen, intestines, liver and gallbladder using positions **6** and **7**. Also treat using positions **3**, **4** and **10**.

## Recommended complementary treatment
• Avoid being constipated, if necessary by taking a herbal laxative.
• When you have a migraine eat soft food that is easy to digest and avoid food rich in fat.
• Put icepacks on the base of the head and the forehead, and soak the feet in hot water; this will sometimes abort a migraine attack.
• Meditate daily, especially focusing on what is your feeling each day.
• Seek counselling or a safe environment where you can release your emotions regularly. When you consciously have held back on the expression of emotions that you consider negative, such as anger, sadness and grief, you will also find you have held back on the positive ones as well.
• Make room for expression. Write a journal about your feelings. It will be a space to write out what is inside you.
• Take vigorous outdoor exercise daily such as brisk walking or cycling five times a week. Fresh air and sunshine will contribute greatly to feeling open and free.
• Play a game you enjoy that is not competitive. Look for win–win situations.
• Have a chiropractic adjustment of back and spine.

# STRESS

According to allopathic medicine, stress is a response to an internal or external stimulus; to some extent it is required to keep us alive. Stimuli evoke the stress response (fight or flight) which prepares a person physically and mentally to respond to potentially harmful events. Chemicals are released which increase heart rate, blood pressure, metabolism and physical activity. Stress becomes a problem when it is persistent, affecting a person's well-being and health. Most common stresses in people's lives are life events such as changes in employment and housing, death or loss of loved ones, or illness. Continued exposure to stressful events can lead to physical and emotional problems such as anxiety, depression, indigestion, muscle aches and heart problems. Another product of excessive stress can be a stomach ulcer. Treatment for stress includes avoidance of stressful stimuli, counselling, rest and planned relaxation periods.

According to natural healing methods, stress is another word for fear. It is often a low-level fear maintained chronically over time. Stress causes the instinctive fight or flight response. Often people feel they must endure or cope with stress in their lives, as it is inappropriate to run away or to fight with someone. They hold steadfast and this results in stress mounting up. When stress becomes chronic the entire body can break down. Stress is the single, largest factor in causing illness in the body, mind and spirit.

## Glands
Adrenals

## Chakras
*Solar Plexus* Affirmation – 'I am a powerful, expressive and open human being'

## Emotional cause
While stress can be positive in that it stimulates the creative side of ourselves and causes us to manifest what we want in our lives, it can also be harmful if not kept at a reasonable level. Stress occurs when we react to situations in our lives

and often blame others for what has happened to us. We may feel that we are the only people who are properly qualified to carry out a project. We get our ego into it and cut off the healthy expression of our tension. There is a need to look within ourselves and question our reactions and where we place the blame. Also, when will you allow yourself to deeply relax?

## Reiki treatment
Treat the adrenal glands using positions **12** and **13**. Use position **18** to stimulate the immune system. You can also use position **30** to treat shock.

## Recommended complementary treatment
• Avoid eating animal fat and protein, coffee and tea, and fried and fatty foods which depress the immune system.
• Walk in nature to help you relax, especially in woods or by the sea.
• Participate in sports such as tennis, racquetball, volleyball or basketball.
• Ride a bicycle four to five times a week.
• Take warm baths with lavender oil to relax.
• Have therapeutic massage, acupressure or shiatsu massage.
• Do breathing exercises to centre you and relax.
• Go and see shows that will make you laugh.
• Meditate, pray and surrender.

# SOMETHING ABOUT MYSELF

**I have a passion** about the work that I do because it promotes making wise choices for peace. What is important to me is that we can experience peace inside ourselves by reconnecting to our spiritual divinity. Once we have experienced this reconnection, our life is enhanced and it becomes natural to share this with others. Therefore the process of making peace in the world starts with the individual first.

As a little girl I saw the world through entirely different eyes. Trees had their own colours beside green. The wind had its song. I was in kinship with all that surrounded me. My father was in the US Air Force so until I was in the fourth grade we were stationed in many places. I met people with different skin colours and languages. The tapestry of my life was full and rich. I had a deep and personal experience with God as I saw him and her.

Then there was a junction in the road, and in a moment it seemed I walked away from the freedom and ease in which I lived my life, and chose a harder way. My reactions to certain circumstances offered me the choice of staying open or to close. I became a closed, unhappy girl. After living this way for some time, I forgot about my previous experiences. I ceased to remember that there was any light in me or around me. I was the one who sat on the outside of life looking in. Afraid to participate, afraid of rejection, I chose to play it safe by not feeling. I escaped into my head and out of my body.

Most of the time I would have welcomed dying, as it would have been a relief from the pain and struggle.

I realise that my story is not much different from that of many others. We have all experienced pain and made choices in life. All decisions are big to those who have chosen, as are the reasons for the choices we have made. What is unique perhaps is that I found a way to come home. But I am getting ahead of the story.

I had many childhood illnesses; my throat became a constant problem and as I entered into puberty my problems accelerated. I was plagued with female and emotional problems. I had few friends. I looked for love in all the wrong places. I reached out to others in desperation to make me complete. There was an empty space in my psyche that eluded being fulfilled. I ran way from my family and my problems. I felt misunderstood and unloved. I married young, at eighteen, to someone socially unacceptable to my family. I had had a miracle pregnancy and two miraculous near-death experiences by the time I was twenty-two. I crawled back into life and yet even that was not enough to shake me awake. I established a pattern for living that involved pain and separation. I chose again, only this time it was a suicide attempt, divorce and running away again. One of the greatest wake-up calls given to me was the pain of having my child kidnapped from me. Life was knocking at my door and I continued to say no.

Looking back on my life I am amazed that I had such staying power and how hard I chose life to be.

I married again and found a new way to see life up close. I opened, trusted and loved, and it ended in divorce. The pain of that was almost enough to wake up, almost but not enough. I had major health problems. I lost mobility in my body; I would fall on the floor when standing up and lost the feeling in my legs. The doctors were not too hopeful about my prognosis. It was around then that I encountered Reiki for the first time. It was another moment that life gave me and the difference this time was I said 'Yes'! Sometimes we have to experience being at rock bottom with no perceivable way out to be ready for change. I had had enough of wallowing in self-pity and disharmony. I wanted more in my life.

I experienced a profound peace inside me. It was as if God had come and taken me by the hand and brought me home. It was not an instant process. It took time to unravel the noes in my life and replace them with yeses. Reiki was my constant companion and has been for many years. The light of my heart was rekindled. This light of love and peace continues to shine for me to see my way home to my heart. Over the years I have recovered fully from my back problem, and the beauty and majesty of the human spirit have touched me.

I moved to Europe in 1989. I left everything behind me as I stepped out into the world. I literally came away from everything safe to discover a deeper sense of my self and a truer purpose for living. I was not on the outside looking in any more; I had chosen to play right in the middle of life. I started teaching Reiki in the UK and the Netherlands, and then I moved to Czechoslovakia in 1991. Another adventure in living began. I kept responding to life, saying yes. The International Association of Reiki was founded in 1990 in Scotland and was moved to the Czech Republic in 1992. There were more opportunities given by life and more yes answers as I responded to this country's people who were just experiencing freedom. What a precious gift they have been to me and what beautiful life lessons they have taught me. As I write this story I am touched to look back at the journey and see so many turns in the road all leading back to me. Thank you Reiki. I have taught over 30,000 students from almost every country in the world. Truly we are a brother-hood, a loving family of humankind.

As I have travelled this beautiful world I have come into contact with the magic again, the magic that I experienced in my childhood. The wind sings its song, the trees are in different colours and hues, and people from many countries have joined with me to become co-creators of peace. It starts with us and then ripples from us, touching others. We have surrendered into the energy of Reiki and together we acknowledge our differences and celebrate the sameness. I invite you to make a wise choice and join us.

For more information about Mari, the International Association of Reiki, or the courses she teaches, you can contact her directly at:

International Association of Reiki spol.s.r.o.
Lesni 14, 46001 Liberec 1, Czech Republic
Tel +420 48 271 0512
Fax +420 48 271 0515
E-mail: reiki@pvtnet.cz
http://www.wisechoices.com

# GLOSSARY OF COMPLEMENTARY METHODS

The following is a list and a brief description of some of the complementary therapies that are recommended in this book. It is important to seek the advice of a qualified practitioner in these fields.

## ACUPRESSURE

Acupressure is a Japanese system of healing that is derived from the precepts of Chinese medicine. Acupressure is based on the principles of acupuncture, but uses the fingers and hands instead of needles. Practitioners apply pressure on pressure points that lie along fourteen energy pathways or meridian lines to restore the vital life force. Along these meridians life force energy or Ki flows. On these meridians exist more than a thousand acupuncture/acupressure points, or generators for this energy. An acupressurist stimulates these points to activate energy along the meridian and to specific organs to bring about healing. There is also a body-mind acupressure that is used called Jin Shin Do bodymind acupressure. It incorporates traditional Japanese acupressure, classic Chinese acupuncture theory, a Taoist yogic philosophy and a Reichian segmented breathing theory. It is often referred to as 'the way of the compassionate spirit'.

# ACUPUNCTURE

Acupuncture is part of a 5,000-year-old Chinese system of harmonising the body. The system of acupuncture uses fine needles to modulate and stimulate tiny points on the meridians to promote the flow of Ki along the meridian to specific organs and tissues of the body, thus returning the system to harmony.

# AROMATHERAPY

Aromatherapy, which traces its origins back to Egypt, India, Babylon, Greece, Rome and the Arab Empire, uses essential oils derived from plants and flowers to heal. The fragrance relaxes, resolves inner conflict and assists in healing. Each essential oil contains its own distinct smell that stimulates an array of emotional, psychological and physical responses. Aromatherapists say that these emotional and psychological states give rise to physical responses, which in turn heal the body. The practice of aromatherapy has only recently become popular in the modern Western world.

# BACH FLOWER THERAPY

Dr Edward Bach (1886–1936) was a British physician who believed that illness is caused by negative emotions. He maintained that certain flower essences have the capacity to overcome specific negative emotions, thereby restoring mental and physical balance. He developed 38 flower remedies and one remedy that uses a combination of flower essences to use in an emergency named Rescue Remedy. This gentle and natural therapy is very effective for treating the presenting emotions, and works on the essential cause of an illness. It treats each person individually. As one layer of the emotion is brought into harmony another may surface. The person being treated is gently brought back into a harmonised state.

# BOWEN BODY THERAPY

Bowen body therapy was developed in Australia sometime after World War Two by Tom Bowen, an industrial chemist. This method uses precise and gentle movements over the facia of the muscle to open the energy to the body. According to some Bowen practitioners, it is likened to a gentle plucking of a guitar string, over certain patterns of tendons, nerves and muscle facia. It sets up a vibration that imparts new information to the body and releases a cascade of neuromuscular reflexes. In turn these reflexes free joints, relax muscles and improve circulation of blood, lymph and energy. It balances the function of the organs. It is like turning on a light switch. The belief is that once the energy has been opened, the body in its innate wisdom will heal itself. The use of Bowen therapy gradually changes the body's structural and functional relationships. People have experienced miraculous results from one or two treatments. Seemingly impossible problems such as frozen shoulders, legs and hip problems that nearly rendered people unable to walk, function with ease. Bowen therapy is also used on horses and dogs.

# CHINESE MEDICINE

Chinese medicine is thought to be over 3,000 years old and is based on a philosophical system that unifies the human being with nature in the widest sense. Health is a state of balance between opposites and wholeness, and is a condition in which all parts of the human psyche find their place of harmony. In such a condition we are fully able to understand and love ourselves and embrace everyone else in life. The major components of Chinese medicine are chi, yin and yang, the five elements comprising wood, fire, earth, metal and water, meridians and acu-points. In treating patients, doctors of Chinese medicine try to affect these aspects by means of herbs, needles, massage, lifestyle recommendations, diet, movement, arts and breathing exercises. The system comprises diet, exercise and meditation. It works with the five elements and the meridians in the body.

**Chi** – the Chinese deal with energy that moves through the body which is invisible in structure and form. It is called chi, energy that flows in its own circulatory pattern. The chi that we possess comes to us through two different sources. We inherit our original genetic chi from our parents: this is the ancestral force over which we have no control and this deter- mines everything from eye colour to body shape. We also have acquired chi that comes from the food, water and air that we take in. We can regulate this by sleeping, breathing, exercise, food and our behaviour.

**Yin and yang** – this is from Chinese Taoism and represents balance between excessive and deficient chi. It is the central concept that pervades traditional Chinese medicine and philosophy. The object of various healing arts and spiritual practices within Chinese medicine is to find the middle way along the physical, emotional and mental extremes.

**The five elements** – yin and yang further divide into five elements or phases of energy: wood, fire, earth, metal and water. The entire universe consists of these elements. Each element also has flavours, sounds, seasons, organs, emotions, colour direction and weather conditions that correspond to it. These are referred to as qualities or ideas. They represent forces of influence. Thus, if you burn wood you will create fire, which will result in ashes, or earth, from which you can mine metal, which when heated becomes molten, like water, which is necessary for the growth of plants and wood. You have then come full circle.

**Meridians** – chi flows through invisible channels called meridians. They are like highway systems that connect towns from one coast to another. The most important are the twelve major channels associated with the twelve major organ systems, plus two vessels called the governing and conception vessels. These vessels oversee all the others.

**Acu-points** – these are small energy centres that are generally sensitive to pressure. There are several ways to either drain excess or activate deficient chi: insertion of fine needles (acupuncture); application of pressure (acupressure); or slow burning of a herb (mugwort) to produce heat (moxabustion).

# CHIROPRACTIC

Daniel Palmer (1845–1913) was a self-taught therapist. He developed chiropractic manipulation in the late 19th century. His belief was that subluxations or misalignments of the vertebrae of the spinal column caused disease. The misalignments can affect nerves resulting in physical dysfunction. Chiropractors focus on adjusting the bones that form the spine, generally through physical manipulation to promote a healthy body.

# DANCE MOVEMENT THERAPY

Practitioners use movement and dance to help people experience and express inner feelings and to resolve conflicts. This practice is especially helpful for people recovering from addiction, disabilities, sexual abuse and long-standing emotional problems.

# EXERCISE

Studies show that moderate exercise boosts the immune system and promotes a sense of well-being. Any exercise that involves the legs, such as walking or cycling, improves circulation because the legs act as auxiliary pumps. Exercise also helps to dissolve blood clots throughout the body and improves the efficiency of the heart as it increases the amount of oxygen that flows to the cells of the body. Walking, running, cycling, swimming, stretching and toning exercise all promote a mind that is more still.

# HERBAL MEDICINE

Long before there was a pharmaceutical industry there were traditional healers who understood how to use plants to help people overcome disease. This is the basis for herbal medicine. Herbs are medicinal plants. Various parts of the plants – the leaves, stems, roots and seeds – are used for their specific healing properties. They are synergetic in nature. Herbalists, rather than concentrating on the individual chemical components of the plant, place their focus on how the herbs work together as a compound. Many herbs contain dozens of active constituents that combine to give the plant its therapeutic value. Herbalists believe that the full plant itself and even certain parts of the plant provide more effective natural medicine. Herbs should be used with discrimination. Some are to be ingested; others brewed as a tea or used as a poultice. It is essential that you consult a person trained in this field if you intend to try herbal remedies.

# HOMOEOPATHY

Dr Samuel Hahnemann (1755–1843), a German physician, developed homoeopathy based on the principle of 'like cures like'. He married two Greek words together to describe his work, *homos*, which means like, and *pathos*, meaning pathology or illness. This law of similars was one of several principles on which he based his new medicine. His contention was that administering minute doses of natural substances that would cause illness in a healthy individual actually treats disease. The goal of homoeopathy is to rid the body of toxins and restore balance to the body and mind. The law of similars was not a new thought to Hahnemann, but was central to the medical approaches used by Hippocrates in 400 BC and by Ayurvedic physicians 2,000 years earlier.

# HYDROTHERAPY

Hydrotherapy quite literally is water therapy that harnesses the healing properties of water. This therapy takes many forms, including massage in or under the water, aerobic or stretching exercises performed in the water, soaking in hot springs, use of steam vapours and revitalising hot, cold or alternating shower sprays. It has long been a part of European healing traditions, where it formed the core of spa cures.

# NATUROPATHY

Benedict Lust developed naturopathic medicine in the late 19th century. Lust was a German-born medical doctor who looked at alternative ways to then common medical approaches of prescribing toxic drugs and using surgery. He felt there could be a more natural approach to patient care. The naturopathic doctor treats patients with therapies drawn from the fields of nutrition, herbal remedies, homoeopathy, physical exercise, acupuncture, hydrotherapy and a variety of bodywork techniques. Naturopathy is a valid course of study in most western European countries.

# NUTRITION

There are many approaches to nutrition. Food combining, low fat and high fibre diets can all be beneficial. For the purposes of this book the nutritional approach recommended is one closely aligned with an aspect of Chinese medicine, namely macrobiotics. The aim is to achieve balance in one's diet. Generally it involves eating foods that are cultivated locally and avoiding processed foods. Macrobiotic diets emphasise eating wholegrains, beans, seeds, nuts, vegetables, fruits and fish. It states that red meat, dairy products and sugar cause imbalance to the body. While I am not suggesting you must adhere to a macrobiotic diet to promote your health, I believe that studying the approach to macrobiotic eating is beneficial, as it is an all-encompassing eating plan, some of which you could incorporate into your own dietary programme.

# PHYSICAL THERAPY

Physical therapy is aimed at the promotion of health and recovery from disabling conditions such as accidents, surgery, sprains, fractures, strokes and neurological disorders. Physical therapists use a broad range of therapeutic modalities, including massage, exercise and electrical stimulation. Their principal goal is to facilitate movement. Some physical therapists specialise in particular areas, for instance occupationally related disorders (such as repetitive strain injury), sports injury or paediatric therapy.

## SHIATSU

The goal of Shiatsu massage is to balance the flow of vital life energy or ki in the body. Shiatsu is used to prevent illness as well as to relieve acute and chronic conditions. Working along the meridian lines, pressure is applied to various points. Gentle stretching can also be used. Shiatsu is often thought of as massage with acupressure.

## T'AI CHI CHUAN

T'ai chi is an ancient Chinese Taoist martial arts practice used to unite the body and mind. Sometimes it is referred to as meditation in motion. T'ai chi integrates mental forces, awareness of breath and slow, graceful movements. It is used to introduce relaxation and to promote health. It is an excellent meditative practice and can be done anywhere. There are sets of routines that you use. I highly recommend this practice as a way to promote a harmonious mind and body. It is a very good way to relieve stress and become centred.

## VISUALISATION THERAPY

This approach to healing uses visualisations or relaxed guided meditations to help an individual imagine a desired condition, such as good health. It is also effective for identifying and removing blockages to this process, thus freeing the mind to create a more healthy environment for healing.

# VITAMIN AND MINERAL THERAPY

Supplements can play an important part in healing. It is recommended that minimum dose of the daily-required vitamins and minerals come from our food. When that is not possible it may be necessary to take supplements to boost the immune system. Consult a Naturopath, Nutrionist or medical doctor/practitioner.

# YOGA

Yoga describes a variety of practices developed in ancient India to unify the body and mind. Most commonly it involves a series of stretching postures, breathing exercises and meditative practices. Yoga attempts to calm the mind and tone the body to create a state of balance in which higher aspects of consciousness can be accessed.

# BIBLIOGRAPHY

## Food and Nutrition

Castleman, M. 1996. *Nature's Cures*. Rodale Press.

Colbin, A. 1986. *Food and Healing, What You Eat Determines Your Health, Your Wellbeing and the Quality of Your Life*. Ballantine Books.

Haas, M.D., E. 1992. *Staying Healthy with Nutrition*. Celestial Arts.

Mindell, E. 1982. *The Vitamin Bible, How the Right Vitamins and Minerals can Revolutionize Your Life*. Arlington Book Publishers.

Pitchford, P. 1993. *Healing with Whole Foods*. North Atlantic Books.

Vogel, H.C.A. 1990. *The Nature Doctor*. Mainstream Publishing Company.

## Energy

Ball, J. 1993. *Understanding Disease*. C.W. Daniel.

Brennan, B. 1998. *Hands of Light, a Guide to Healing through the Energy Field*. Bantam Books.

Chuen, Master L.K. 1991. *The Way of energy*. Gaia Books.

Claire T. 1995. *Bodywork, What Type of Massage to Get, and How to Make the Most of It*. William Morrow and Company.

Gawain, S. 1982. *Creative Visualization*. New World Library. San Rafael.

Hall, M. 1997. *Practical Reiki, a Practical Step by Step Guide to This Ancient Healing Art*. Thorsons/HarperCollins.